Cost Containment
in Higher Education

Issues and Recommendations

Walter A. Brown, Cayo Gamber

ASHE-ERIC Higher Education Report: Volume 28, Number 5
Adrianna J. Kezar, Series Editor

Prepared and published by

JOSSEY-BASS
A Wiley Company
San Francisco

In cooperation with

ERIC Clearinghouse on Higher Education
The George Washington University
URL: www.eriche.org

Association for the Study
of Higher Education
URL: www.tiger.coe.missouri.edu/~ashe

Graduate School of Education and Human Development
The George Washington University
URL: www.gwu.edu

Cost Containment in Higher Education: Issues and Recommendations
Walter A. Brown, Cayo Gamber
ASHE-ERIC Higher Education Report: Volume 28, Number 5
Adrianna J. Kezar, Series Editor

This publication was prepared partially with funding from the Office of Educational Research and Improvement, U.S. Department of Education, under contract no. ED-99-00-0036. The opinions expressed in this report do not necessarily reflect the positions or policies of OERI or the Department.

ISSN 0884-0040   electronic ISSN 1536-0709   ISBN 0-7879-5838-7

The ASHE-ERIC Higher Education Report is part of the Jossey-Bass Higher and Adult Education Series and is published six times a year by Wiley Subscription Services, Inc., a Wiley company, at Jossey-Bass, 989 Market Street, San Francisco, California 94103-1741.

For subscription information, see the Back Issue/Subscription Order Form in the back of this journal.

Prospective authors are strongly encouraged to contact Adrianna Kezar at (301) 405-0868 or kezar@wam.umd.edu.

Visit the Jossey-Bass Web site at **www.josseybass.com.**

Printed in the United States of America on acid-free recycled paper containing 100 percent recovered waste paper, of which at least 20 percent is postconsumer waste.

Executive Summary

Institutions of higher learning have been and continue to be influenced by a variety of internal and external factors as they attempt to justify and contain their costs. It has become commonplace for policy makers on the federal and the state level, along with concerned members of the general public, to voice their concerns about the increasingly high price of attaining a college education. As a result, private and public colleges and universities have been called upon to justify their current expenditures and are being held accountable for successfully devising and implementing budgetary practices and cost saving initiatives. The value and applicability of these practices and initiatives can be more fully understood when expenditures are contextualized by evaluating those internal and external factors that drive the costs and impact the budgets.

Internal costs account for over 60 percent of the total expenditures in four-year private and public institutions. Those expenditures include instructional costs, academic support, student services, facility management, and institutional research. In order to evaluate how resources are expended in each area, one must evaluate how each area is important to the operation of the institution as a whole, how the area might benefit from recognizing current trends, how adopting cost containment efforts currently in use in the private sector might prove beneficial, and how adopting cost containment strategies currently in use in other institutions of higher learning might prove worthwhile. External factors also impinge on a wide variety of budgetary practices and cost containment efforts. For example, such external factors as academic program mandates from state-level higher-education governing boards, the repeated call for accountability measures within the higher-education community, state assessment models, market forces, and the very budgetary process itself influence both costs and efforts to contain those costs. In order to become more cost efficient, universities and colleges need to evaluate how to respond to the impact of both internal and external factors and internal and external forces.

Some of the major questions that university administrators—including academic officers, program officers, and fiscal officers—need to address are

1. What has been the trend of cost increases associated with prescribed expenditures over the last five-year period?
2. How essential is a given expenditure to the operation of the university?
3. What have been successful cost saving strategies used by other four-year institutions and by corporations?
4. What are the issues associated with a given expenditure currently and what are the issues projected to be associated with a given expenditure in the future?
5. What practices have been recommended for the effective financial management of institutions of higher learning; moreover, what performance measures have been used to indicate that such practices are called for and are open to replication?
6. What impact do state governing bodies have on their institutions' cost containment efforts?

The majority of the current research on cost containment is devoted to discussions of policy, philosophical deliberations, or grand principles rather than to comprehensive delineations of how to apply specific recommendations or best practices. It is clear that much more is needed in order to understand and implement concrete operations that will result in greater cost efficiency. Given that there are not numerous examples of best practices in academia, many university administrators have looked to those ventures, such as in the business world, where the management and allocation of scarce resources has been implemented successfully. Consequently, many university administrators have modeled their containment practices on major corporations—including corporate practices of outsourcing, decentralization, and capital planning—to become more cost efficient. As a result, the effectiveness of using the corporate sector as a model and of borrowing the best practices recommended by the business sector needs to be scrutinized.

Clearly there are advantages and disadvantages to pursuing a specific course of action to contain costs. For example, while it is believed by many that the tenure system is inflexible and taxes the financial operations of the university, some economists believe that the tenure system has controlled costs. These economists believe that colleges and universities actually save funds in the long run through the retention of tenured faculty because the salary levels of tenured faculty are maintained at a lower rate over the years (when compared to the earning opportunities in the private sector) in exchange for the security in employment that tenure offers. Some researchers also have argued that post-tenure reviews can be imposed to ensure that tenured faculty remain productive and accountable. In addition, while many would argue that employment of part-time faculty allows the institution to cut instructional costs, as more part-time faculty seek to unionize, collective-bargaining agreements will dramatically influence the cost-saving potential of employing adjuncts.

In addressing cost-savings initiatives related to academic support, a good portion of the university or college's attention is focused on academic libraries, because libraries constitute the major financial investment within academic support services. The acquisition costs of both print and electronically delivered information have risen dramatically. Upgrading and maintaining technology also functions as an ongoing expenditure both in its use in acquiring publications and in its use in the very operations of the library system. Thus, to reduce costs, administrators should consider the worthiness of implementing outsourcing or developing consortium efforts in their library operations.

Another internal factor to consider is how the financial pressure to maintain plant operations and facilities has become a pronounced concern at most institutions of higher learning. As a general rule, during the fiscal crises of the 1980s, university administrators sacrificed the upkeep of facilities in order to reallocate resources to academic programs that were in danger of shutting down. As a result, colleges and universities tended to neglect critical upkeep in plant operations and facilities in an effort to realize short-term costs savings. Thus, universities now are faced with ensuring they can cover a wide array of expenditures not usually covered in the annual operations budget, including deferred maintenance, capital renewal and replacement, facilities remodeling and renovation, retrofitting for energy conservation, elimination of safety problems, provisions for the accessibility for persons with disabilities, and compliance with local, state, and federal regulatory requirements. Therefore, it has become critical that administrators implement a strategic planning process that provides a critical review of how plant and facility operations contribute to the mission of the university, and of how to identify internal and external issues that could affect cost containment opportunities. Higher-education institutions also need to weigh the potential costs associated with self-operation as compared to the costs of outsourcing. In addition, given that for the majority of universities and colleges, the aggregate electric power bill has been the second largest operating expense next to faculty and staff salaries, administrators need to be cognizant of the possible affects of deregulation of electrical energy.

One of the growing concerns related to research costs is how state, government, and private funding are exerting more and more control over university decisions—at all levels—vis a vis research venues and ventures. There are growing concerns that soon external constituencies will determine the direction of faculty research. Currently, research costs are impacted by public perceptions, internal costs, federal policies, and entrepreneurial enticements. It has become a point of public concern that many faculty members regard research as their highest priority because it is through research that most faculty members can maintain or increase the prestige of their institutions. Moreover, the financial well-being of many institutions of higher learning is tied to the institution's ability to attract outside research funding. Competition for funds has been heightened and, in turn, has prompted a shift in the types of research being conducted. This shift is characterized, in large part, by a turn from basic curiosity-driven research to research that is more strategic or commercial in nature. This change in the types of research being conducted has caused many to question what incentives should guide academic research. There also are ongoing concerns about earmarked federal research funds. In addition, there are increasing concerns that if academic researchers develop financial connections to industry, they may discover that such connections will interfere with the kinds of independent inquiry that have been expected from institutions of higher learning. As a result, there have been calls to hold faculty members and their institutions more accountable for how research funds are used and for demonstrating the integrity of the institution's ongoing relationship with its students.

In addition to the aforementioned internal factors and forces, student services are vital to the survival of a college or university because it is the recruitment and retention of students that determine the future of the academy. However, while it may be that the growth in student services came about when the competition for students was its most intense, it also is true that when budgets are cut, student services often are the hardest hit. A wide array of factors influence student-service expenditures—from attending to federal statutes and regulations (such as the civil rights codes, the First Amendment, the Americans with Disabilities Act, financial aid, and sexual harassment regulations) to evaluating an institution's commitment to need-based aid or merit aid.

While the aforementioned internal factors must be evaluated in terms of how to implement cost saving initiatives, there also are external factors to consider. Four-year public institutions, in particular, are impacted by external forces outside of the sphere of their control. For example, the financial health of state institutions is intimately tied to the economic well-being of the state where they reside. In addition, the budgets proposed by the legislators for state universities contain recommendations that have cost implications for each of their institutions of higher learning. State universities are confronted with a variety of problems when they must compete for their share of the revenue with other sectors (such as primary and secondary schools or correction facilities). In order to better align their budget requests with efficiency and effectiveness, more and more states are moving toward some form of performance-based budgeting. Such performance-based budgeting efforts also attempt to acknowledge the public outcry for greater accountability in higher education.

Finally, a review of the literature reveals that more empirical research is needed to best evaluate the actual experiences of individual institutions and the best practices those institutions have developed and implemented in order to encourage greater cost efficiency. Perhaps it is due to the discretion institutions of higher learning practice concerning revealing internal information about their finances and operations, and perhaps it is due as well to a lack of venues for publication, nonetheless, it is clear that a great deal could be gained were there more widely publicized discussions of the actual practice(s) of containing costs at specific institutions. While various reports and case studies are engaging and informative in their efforts to address financing higher education, it often is difficult to determine how successful various efforts have been as there are few long-term, quantitative or qualitative studies conducted that confirm whether the efforts made to contain costs have achieved their objectives and whether those efforts could be duplicated productively at other institutions. Thus, more research is needed that assesses the efficacy of individual institutions and of collective practices associated with containing the rising costs of higher education.

Contents

Foreword

In contrast with the economic constraint of the late 1970s and early 1980s, the 1990s represented a time of growth and increasing budgets for most campuses. The generally positive economic conditions resulted in few campuses having to contemplate cost savings strategies or face hard decisions such as closing down programs. However, public concern over accountability and costs of higher education increased during the 1990s, with many legislatures asking campuses to defend their expenses. In addition to this external concern related to campus costs, the pendulum has swung back to recession and the economic outlook is poor. The events of September 11 will have longstanding effects on campuses. Fundraising will most likely be less fruitful. Government resources will be shifted to different priorities. Campuses once again find themselves searching for approaches to examining their expenses and revenues and are focused on ways to capitalize new revenue generation and to make strategic cost savings.

Older books on the topic of cost containment will be inappropriate to guide current decision making. Operations have changed on college campuses due to the increased reliance on technology; growth of the profit sector and information resources; demands for accountability and assessment; new employment contracts; and legislation about equity, among other environmental changes. Clearly, the world in which administrators must make budgetary decisions has changed. Brown and Gamber's issue could not be published in a timelier era.

In *Cost Containment in Higher Education: Issues and Recommendations,* Brown and Gamber, of The George Washington University, offer sound advice for administrators in this new era of low returns on investment and greater competition. Brown spent part of his career in the corporate sector working for companies such as PepsiCo and Avon; these experiences provide him with an innovative approach to university budgeting. The focus of this issue is on ways that college campuses can examine their budgets to make needed modifications that align with their mission and goals. This issue synthesizes research on internal cost containment strategies across the institution from salaries to libraries to facilities and deferred maintenance. Case studies are presented to provide context for suggested strategies and to illustrate how implementation may differ based on the campus culture and environment. Few books provide the detailed analysis of campus budgets or the strategic advice offered by Brown and Gamber. Evidence about effective translation of business models to higher education is a main theme, based on the authors' experience with corporate approaches. This issue also highlights approaches from business and industry that have not been implemented in higher education, but show promise. Although many principles cannot be translated with success to campuses, it is important to remain open to innovation from other contexts.

Other recent ASHE-ERIC monographs may be useful for campus administrators searching for resources to guide decision making during this difficult time period. Sutton and Bergerson's *Faculty Compensation Systems* is important for making decisions about the largest budget item on every campus. Because salary decisions are related to morale and motivation, it is important to understand some of the psychological and sociological costs of decisions related to salaries. Cantor's *Higher Education Outside the Academy* can assist administrators in understanding more about the for-profit environment and suggests ways to develop strategic alliances to supplement revenue generation. *Enrollment Management for the 21st Century*, by Penn, describes ways campuses can attract and retain more students, an important aspect of revenue generation.

In the difficult times ahead, thoughtful innovation and experimentation will distinguish those who succeed. Successful institutions are defined here as those that remain financially solvent while maintaining their mission and commitment to educational integrity.

Adrianna J. Kezar
ASHE-ERIC Series Editor
University of Maryland

Introduction

BOTH FEDERAL AND STATE government policy makers, along with concerned members of the public, have been critical of the increasingly high price of attaining a college education. Over the past five years, the percent increase in the average tuition for four-year public and private institutions has increased well above the average percent increases in inflation and in government funding levels for higher education (The National Commission on the Cost of Higher Education, 1998). The levels of increases in tuition vary according to whether an institution is public or private; research, doctoral or liberal arts; or a four-year college or two-year community college.

Private institutions are largely dependent upon revenue from tuition while state colleges and universities are heavily subsidized by state funds. Therefore, in order to examine cost containment strategies, one must factor in reductions in federal research funding and research-funding opportunities along with evidence of an ongoing decline in state appropriations to more fully understand those factors that affect four-year institutions of higher learning (Zemsky and Massy, 1990). In an effort to begin to respond to these concerns, it is vital for university administrators to be cognizant of the factors and attendant research that explain what drives the expenditure base (internally as well as externally), that determine the cost of operating higher education institutions, and that ultimately affect tuition levels (Massy, 1987; Waggaman, 1991).

One of the major internal factors that must be addressed is instructional costs as they constitute over 40 percent of the total expenditures in public and private four-year institutions (*Chronicle Almanac,* 2001). Recently, there also have been discussions regarding how tenure may contribute counterproductively to future cost containment efforts as employment costs (high competitive salaries, health insurance, retirement, sabbatical leave, tuition waivers, housing, and travel allowances) have risen at a rate disproportionate to the institution's ability to cover such expenditures (Chait and Ford, 1982; Diamond, 1994; Gappa, 1984). As a result, many universities are in the process of strategically reexamining their future financial commitment to tenure. Externally, states either have assumed the role as a facilitator of or as a barrier to cost containment. As a facilitator, state legislatures have imposed specific mandates to reduce spending in areas that are not contributing to the university's mission. However, at the same time, state legislators often hold administrators accountable for the performance of academic programs that, in many cases, would call for increases in financial resources in order to ensure their success (Anderson, 1988; Berne and Schramm, 1986).

The first objective of this issue is to synthesize research that outlines those internal cost containment strategies in several key categories that contribute, on average, to over 50 percent of total expenditures in four-year public and private institutions. Those expenditures include instructional costs, academic support, student services, facility management, and institutional research. The second objective of the issue is to examine external factors that could affect cost containment objectives within state institutions. Those areas include academic program mandates from state-level higher-education governing boards, the call for accountability measures within the higher education community, state assessment models, and the budgetary process itself.

The current discourse, as it has been conducted on the public level, the institutional level, and the federal level—from opinion pieces in the *Washington Post* to congressional debates—charges institutions of higher education with becoming more assertive in eradicating inefficiencies and more creative in reducing costs so that their respective institutions remain viable and competitive in the next century. According to a report issued by the Council for Aid to Education, in order to regain public trust, "the higher education sector must systematically address issues of cost, productivity, efficiency, and effectiveness as a prerequisite for increases in public sector investment" (p. 17). In addition, one of the primary recommendations from the 1998 Report of the National Commission on the Cost of Higher Education included the requirement that colleges and universities strengthen institutional cost control. However, while cost containment is highly and widely recommended, it is often discussed in terms of policy, philosophical deliberations, or the application of grand principles. Much more is needed to understand and implement concrete operations. Because there are not numerous examples of concrete, best practices in academia to learn how to control expenditures, many university administrators have looked to those ventures where the management and allocation of scarce resources has been implemented successfully. Consequently, many university administrators have adopted the approaches and strategies of major corporations—including outsourcing, decentralization, and capital planning—in order to become more cost efficient (Vandament, 1989; Hyatt, Shulman, and Santiago, 1984).

> While cost containment is highly and widely recommended, it is often discussed in terms of policy, philosophical deliberations, or the application of grand principles. Much more is needed to understand and implement concrete operations.

This issue is written for university administrators who have been charged with taking an aggressive look at their cost structure in order to discover the most efficient means to control their costs. Academic officers, program officers, and fiscal officers who need to understand the complexity of the university cost structures and at the same time make financial decisions in their respective areas would benefit from the analyses and discussions herein. To that end, this issue focuses on two major views of cost containment: internal factors and external factors. Under internal cost factors, five internal expenditure areas that make up over 60 percent of total expenditures found in four-year public and private institutions will be reviewed. The areas include instructional cost, student services, research, plant operation, and academic support (see Table 1). An examination of each area will cover the financial issues affecting each area, each area's importance to the operation of the institution, how the area might benefit from recognizing current trends, how adopting cost containment strategies currently in use in the private sector or in other institutions of higher

TABLE 1
**Financing of Higher Education Expenditures
(Colleges and Universities)**

Expenditures	Public Institutions	Private Institutions
Instruction	32.1 percent	27.0 percent
Research	10.1	7.7
Public service	4.6	2.4
Academic support	7.6	6.1
Student services	5.0	5.4
Institutional support	9.0	10.6
Plant operation	6.6	6.1
Scholarships & Fellowships	4.4	11.4
Auxiliary enterprises	9.6	8.8
Mandatory transfers	1.2	1.4
Hospitals	9.8	13.1
Total Current Fund Expenditures	100.0 percent	100.0 percent

Source: *Chronicle of Higher Education Almanac, 2001.*

learning might prove beneficial, how financial synthesis and incentives that promote cost savings could be implemented, and when and where efficiencies and demonstration of worth and value occur. Business publications, such as the *Wall Street Journal* and *Harvard Business Review,* consistently highlight cost issues confronting corporations that can be strategically juxtaposed with universities to aid administrators in more fully comprehending personnel, capital expenditures, and administrative costs. In addition, external cost factors will be reviewed to determine how universities and colleges might respond to the impact of market forces, the call for greater accountability and productivity, and the imposition of budgetary constraints upon both public and private institutions. As applicable, we also will present short situational case studies that detail the strategies universities have employed in response to cost containment problems.

A critical approach for this issue is to present literature from both a higher education and a business perspective on cost containment strategies. We concur with William Vandament that "institutional administrators now must master techniques developed in business administration in order to manage financial affairs that are growing increasingly complex" (Vandament, 1989, p. 13). Some of the major questions addressed in this issue are 1) What has been the trend of cost increases associated with prescribed expenditures over the last five-year period? 2) How essential is a given expenditure to the operation of the university? 3) What have been cost saving strategies used by other four-year institutions and corporations? 4) What are the issues associated with this expenditure currently and for the future? 5) What are the recommendations for universities as they relate to effective financial management? 6) What impact do states' governing bodies have on their institutions' cost containment efforts? These questions are guided by our conviction that cost containment in higher education is one of the most critical issues facing colleges and universities in the twenty-first century. To sustain a healthy financial structure, administrators first must have ample knowledge of the internal and external factors that affect cost structures. And then administrators must customize those cost containment strategies that will contribute to the successful financial management of their institution while also maintaining and ensuring its competitive position as an institution of higher learning.

What's Driving Your Instructional Cost?

Faculty Compensation

Instructional costs represent 32.6 percent and 27 percent of total expenditures at public and private four-year institutions, respectively (*Chronicle of Higher Education Almanac,* 2001). The total budgeted costs for full-time tenured and contractual faculty comprise the bulk of university instructional costs. These costs primarily include the professional salaries of faculty, fringe benefits, and graduate assistance funding (American Institute of Certified Public Accountants, 1994). Often private institutions shoulder more of the instructional cost increases than do public institutions. During the 1997-98 and 1998-99 academic periods, average salaries increased 3.3 percent at public institutions and 3.7 percent at private institutions (Clery and Lee, 2000). During the 1998-99 period, the average faculty member earned $54,303, which represented a 3.5 percent increase from the previous academic year of $52,481 (National Center for Educational Statistics, 1999). At doctoral institutions, professors from each rank made considerably more at private institutions than at public doctoral institutions (Hearn, 1999). For example, at the top of the chart, a full professor earned on average $89,028 at a private doctoral institution versus an average of $75,852 at a public doctoral institution (National Center for Educational Statistics, 1999). More recent figures indicate that salaries also vary according to geographical region as well.

California faculty members in public four-year institutions average $67,587—the highest average faculty salary at public four-year institutions: New Jersey faculty members in public four-year *institutions averaged $67,458: The average salary paid to public four-year faculty members exceeded $60,000 in nine states, up five from last year's four. For the first time, no state had an average salary in public four-year institutions below $40,000. Massachusetts faculty members earned the highest average salary among four-year independent institutions ($68,724), Alaska faculty members earned the lowest ($31,547)* (National Education Association, 2000).

Among disciplines, professors who teach in the areas of Law and Legal Studies, Business Management, and Administrative Services, on average, have salaries higher than all other disciplines.

In the 1970s and 1980s, a primary cost concern involved increases in the average cost of fringe benefits as a percentage of faculty salaries (Chronister and Kepple, 1987). During the 1970-71 period, fringe benefits made up 10.2 percent of average faculty salaries. In 1982-83, the percentage rose to 16.2 percent (American Council on Education, 1984). The increment was primarily a result of rising health care benefits and social security taxes. Those same concerns were more pronounced in the 1990s. In comparing the 1989-90 period with 1993-94, the growth in average benefit costs exceeded average salary increases by 26 percent versus 16 percent. In 1994, the increase represented 25.2 percent of the average total salary (Chronister, 1996).

More current data reveals much of the same upward movement in average benefit costs. Connecting the 1990-91 period with 1997-98 in current dollars, the average benefit costs increased at a faster rate (25.4 percent) than the increase in average faculty salaries (23.4 percent) (Chronister, 2000). During the same period, benefit costs in current dollars increased by 30 percent at independent institutions and by 24 percent at public institutions. In 1997-98 the average benefit costs represented 24 percent of total salary. Within those benefit costs, retirement (9.7 percent), medical insurance (5.8 percent), and social security (6.1 percent) made up the largest portion of the contribution (American Association of University Professors, 1998).

Changes in the health care provider environment over the years have also had an impact on administrative costs for faculty and staff. At least 85 percent of those workers in the United States who participate in health care plans are in some form of managed care program (Employee Benefits Research Institute, 1998). "Since 1993, reports EBRI, employers moved employees into managed care plans, expanded utilization of active workers, increased premium costs-sharing with personnel, and reduced or ended retiree health benefits" (Chronister, 1996, p. 84). In addition, employers in both the public and private sectors have been shifting workers to less expensive managed care systems in an effort to reduce their employee health care costs. Workers also are being required to pay a larger contribution for their health care benefits. This requirement was clearly evidenced during the period between 1991 and 1997, when the proportion of contributions paid by employees increased from 49 percent to 69 percent (Bureau of Labor Statistics, 1999).

More recent economic indicators in the private sector, such as those cited in the Employment Cost Index, highlight employer costs in wages and salaries and show an increase of 0.9 percent between the third and fourth quarters of 1999 (Delano, 2000). This increase was driven by a 1.3 percent increase in benefit costs. Furthermore, heath care costs for both the public and private sectors are expected to increase in the future due to the following market conditions:

- Mandated state benefits have increased between 1970 and 1996, increasing the cost for fully inured plans.
- HMO consolidation is attempting to reduce competition in many markets that could eventually drive up costs. For example, in Texas, Aetna would have controlled 64 percent of the Houston HMO market if it had not been required to sell the NYLC are HMO business.
- The provider community has reorganized itself through mergers and acquisitions, which will translate into higher prices. In addition, physicians are pushing to join unions to take advantage of the collective bargaining process in their efforts to win higher wages (Carlson, 2000).

Further impacts on the cost of managed care programs in the industry will depend on emerging court litigation that challenges cost containment efforts by the health care delivery system. "If courts consistently rule in favor of patients' challenges, it may be difficult to sustain cost containment mechanisms. But if courts rule in favor of cost containment, patients will have little recourse when care is denied, and institutions will feel less constrained in introducing cost containment programs" (Jacobson, 1999, p. 2). And more often than not, when health care providers incur greater costs, they will pass on these costs to the institutions and consumers who use the health care services.

Instructional costs may also increase in the future as a result of collective-bargaining agreements for part-time faculty members and teaching assistants. Across the majority of disciplines, full-time faculty members' average salaries, at four-year public institutions where collective bargaining is in place, are already higher than the average faculty salaries at non-collective bargaining four-year public institutions (College and University Personnel Association, 1997). Organizations such as the American Association of University Professors (AAUP) and the National Education Association (NEA) have come out in favor of collective bargaining for both groups (Leatherman, 1999). The National Labor Relations Board also let stand the decision to allow faculty at a private institution (Manhattan College) to engage in collective bargaining. These opportunities to engage in collective bargaining often may translate into higher salaries and the acquisition of full benefits packages that are not normally offered to part-time faculty (Saltzman, 2000).

> **Opportunities to engage in collective bargaining often may translate into higher salaries and the acquisition of full benefits packages that are not normally offered to part-time faculty (Saltzman, 2000).**

As of 1993, 41 percent of all faculties were classified as part-time. Of this mix, 48 percent were located at the community college level, 4.8 percent were at private liberal arts colleges, 20 percent were in comprehensive colleges and universities, 10.1 percent were in doctorate granting universities, and 9.8 percent were in research universities (Gappa and Leslie, 1997). These figures could be understated because it is difficult to capture the exact contributions made by all part-time faculty. However, the organization of part-time faculty and teaching assistant bargaining groups has started.

NEA, for example, won a 1998 representation election for a bargaining unit of almost 500 part-time faculty at Columbia College in Chicago. A year earlier, more than 1,000 University of Alaska adjuncts voted for American Association of University Professors (AAUP) and American Federation of Teachers (AFT) representation, and nearly 2,000 part timers in New Jersey's state colleges voted for AFT representation.

Organizing activity among TAs increased during the 1990s. University of Iowa voted to organize in 1996. AFT became the bargaining representative for some Wayne State University TAs in 1998; an effort to include the remaining TAs and research assistants followed. TAs and research assistants at the University of Minnesota voted against union representation in 1999. But the United Workers (UAW) won representation election for TAs at UCLA, Berkeley, and six other University of California campuses in 1999, following a systemwide strike in December 1998. In May 1999, the UAW filed a petition for a representation election for TAs at New York University (Saltzman, 2000, p. 43).

In addition to possibly paying more for adjunct labor, a traditional labor source that represents one of the most essential cost savings units, universities and colleges must also now address the fact that they will need to accommodate the ongoing tenure of professors who once would have retired. As a result of federal legislation that eliminated mandatory retirement, tenured professors are now able to work well past the previous mandatory retirement age of 65. Consequently, colleges and universities have had to factor in as part of their instructional costs the probability of older, higher salaried tenured professors remaining over a longer period of time. In an effort to gain a better understanding of these costs institutions are allowed by law to develop incentives for early retirement in the form of compensation packages as options for those senior level tenured faculty members who decide to retire prior to age 65. However, such (cost saving) compensation packages are subject to three conditions:

1. The colleges/universities must not implement any age-based reduction or cessation of benefits other than the supplemental benefits.
2. The age-based benefits offered through voluntary retirement, health care, and other welfare plans must be supplemental to benefits that faculty receive as part of their benefits and compensation package. The benefits should be additional to any retirement or severance benefits available to tenured faculty members, exclusive of early retirement or exit-incentive plans, within the preceding 365 days.
3. Tenured faculty who reach the minimum age and satisfy all non-age-based conditions for receiving supplemental benefits have the option, over a period of 180 days, to retire and receive the same maximum supplemental benefit available to younger, similarly situated employees. The faculty members must be in a position to delay retirement for at least 180 days after making the decision (Chronister, 2000).

These policies do not preclude colleges and universities from being creative in offering tenured faculty members early out packages when they choose to retire between the ages of 65 and 70. Because of the large number of faculty who will become eligible for retirement, institutions in the twenty-first century will have the opportunity to replace higher priced retired professors with lower ranked replacements if they are successful in selling such incentive packages to eligible older faculty (Hearn, 1999).

Faculty Productivity

In both for-profit and nonprofit organizations, personnel or labor costs make up a substantial portion of the operating budget and consequently are easy targets for reduction during uncertain economic periods. As the last few years have shown, even during prosperous economic cycles corporations have carried out draconian reductions in their workforce in an effort to increase earnings for dividend payouts to shareholders. If reductions in the workforce are necessary, it is critical to have substantive information regarding the performance of workers in order to evaluate operating efficiencies. One way to determine efficiencies is to analyze worker productivity levels. In corporations, productivity is measured by examining the financial relationship between inputs and outputs (Hopkins, 1990). The more a firm can produce (outputs) with a given level of inputs, the more productive it is (Bucklin, 1977). Because of the cost factor, the measurement of productivity is extremely important due to the premise that most sectors of the economy, particularly the service and retail sectors, are labor intensive (Brown and Dev, 2000). According to one estimate, labor expenses in the hotel industry account for 40 percent of all operating costs (Shaw, 1988). In the service industry, improving labor productivity is critical, as those gains allow firms to lower costs and subsequently increase their profitability. "This type of productivity can lead to increased demand by offering more services, which can fund new technologies, which in turn, can enhance labor productivity, and thus the cycle of productivity continues. Thus, the productivity of a service firm's labor, as well as its capital, has important implications for its overall marketing strategy, pricing, strategy, cost structure, and profitability" (Brown and Dev, 2000, p. 1).

In higher education, instructional costs are the largest operating expenditure for four-year institutions of higher learning. As mentioned earlier, instructional costs for private and public four-year institutions represent 40 percent and 45 percent, respectively, of the total average expenditures (*Chronicle Almanac of Higher Education,* 2001). Studies dating back to the early 1900s have suggested that high unit costs in higher education have been associated with higher faculty salaries coupled with low teaching loads and smaller class sizes (Clark, 1976). Accordingly, "some major public universities have established minimum enrollment standards to ensure that each class scheduled has a sufficient enrollment to justify the costs incurred in providing the instruction" (State University of New York, 1991, p. 141). However, faculty defines productivity by the number of research publications generated over a specific period. Most faculty balk at the theory of producing at high levels as if they were factory workers, whose increased output would somehow pass on cost savings to the institution (Massy and Wilger, 1995). A current dilemma for colleges and universities is how to best reconcile and measure faculty's definition of

Instructional costs are the largest operating expenditure for four-year institutions of higher learning.

productivity with conventional measures of resource allocation based on the number of academic programs and class size. This issue is compounded by economic and public pressure being exerted on colleges and universities, particularly in public institutions, for more faculty accountability.

Faculty productivity and workloads (how faculty members spend their time) have been questioned by state legislators, governors, and the general public. Such inquiries come in response to reductions in state budgets, competition for other state programs such as health care programs and corrections facilities, K through 12 reform, welfare, and the increased cost of attending colleges and universities (Hines and Highman, 1996; Kennedy, 1995; Layzell, 1996; McGuinnes, 1994). As suggested by one researcher, "Faculty productivity is an estimate of the efficiency and effectiveness of a faculty member in achieving expected professional standards, or designates how well faculty members accomplish their professional responsibilities per unit of resources invested while faculty workload refers to how much a faculty member has to do the total set of activities in the formal and informal job descriptions of a professor" (Allen, 1996, p. 25).

There are several issues involved in measuring faculty productivity and faculty workload. Department chairs have the capability to compute the number of students enrolled in class sessions, the number of scholarly publications, as well as the number of conference presentations and committee memberships, but the intangibles that should also be included in the equation, such as quality and excellence, are missing (Hopkins, 1990). In addition, workloads and productivity vary for faculty depending on the type of institutions and the disciplines. For example, at research universities faculty tend to spend almost half of their time (35–45 percent) engaged in some sort of research activity. At comprehensive institutions, instruction plays a more dominant role in the distribution of workloads (65–75 percent) (Presley and Engelbride, 1998). It also is difficult to quantify productivity and workload for faculty when the time spent preparing for class, presentations, committee work, and community service is also factored in. In addition, the validity of self-reporting data also must be taken into account (Layzell, 1996). Some of this data can be easily inflated to reflect faculty that are already operating at capacity. In addition, "higher education's critics ask why teaching additional courses should not be taken as an indicator of improved faculty productivity. Faculty, on the other hand, see load escalation as producing decreased, not increased, productivity" (Massy and Wilger, 1995, p. 18). Faculty view increased workloads, through additional courses taught or an increase in class size, as a reduction in their discretionary time to do research. Further, a 1995 study on "Improving Productivity" concluded that

> *Faculty associates productivity improvement with measurement. They perceive a heightened emphasis on counting enrollments and publications and worry about the adverse effects on quality. For many faculty, "productivity improvements" means a heavier teaching load and, therefore, less research and diminished educational quality. However, when faculty are faced with choice, they will protect research time at the expense of increased class size* (Massy and Wilger, 1995, p. 20).

This statement implies that large class sizes don't necessarily have an adverse impact on quality of instruction, but that the absence of time devoted toward research activities poses the greatest concern for faculty. Consequently, when faculty are given the choice, they refrain from teaching large classes. This represents the essence of the argument over faculty productivity and cost containment in higher education. University administrators have provided evidence that increases in faculty workload do contribute to lower instructional unit costs (Nyquist, 1970).

Further discussion on productivity should also include the relationship between faculty and instructional productivity. The latter relates directly to activities in the classroom, which could include the use of technology in teaching and learning. Again, it is assumed that there are areas contained in both descriptions, if used to measure total productivity, that are not quantifiable, such as class preparation and social obligations outside of class activities with students (that is informal advising sessions, picnics, sporting events, and so on). This difficulty in quantifying how faculty members spend their time does not mean that administrators are not presented with opportunities to further examine faculty productivity for cost containment purposes. In 1998, the

Maryland Higher Education Commission study found that the Maryland system had the potential to save $34 million if full-time faculty at research and comprehensive institutions in the state met the standard teaching loads of five and eight courses per year, respectively. (Maryland Higher Education Commission, 1998). The dilemmas surrounding the ways in which faculty productivity is evaluated and the ways in which such evaluations affect salaries are clarified in the 1993 study conducted by the National Center on Postsecondary Teaching, Learning, and Assessment. The study found that full-time tenure track salary levels were based on the following scenarios:

- The more time devoted to teaching and instruction, the lower the salary.
- The more time spent in the classroom, the lower the salary of faculty.
- The more time spent doing research, the higher the salary of faculty.
- The more publications faculty had, the higher the salary (Fairweather, 1993 in Layzell).

Traditional recommendations in producing cost savings and ensuring faculty productivity usually involve a combination of the following recommendations:

- Given the ongoing public concerns that inadequate attention is being paid to teaching, many colleges and universities would be advised to require that their faculty spend more time in the classroom teaching larger class sizes (Cohen, 1998). However, it should be noted that this requirement ultimately will sacrifice some portion of research and publication productivity, and yet it can be argued that it also will reduce the need to hire additional faculty to cover those classes (Cohen, 1998).
- Institutions of higher education should eliminate duplication in curriculum by establishing statewide or regional compacts whereby institutions strong in one area attract students from other colleges that can no longer afford to support those programs (Cohen, 1998). This would in effect transfer programs with low enrollments, and that were not covering costs, to institutions operating at efficient program levels. Such transfers could result in greater cost efficiency, as the closure of non-performing programs would free up resources for other programs performing at higher levels of

productivity. In addition, colleges and universities should consider forming consortia whereby students are able to satisfy degree requirements at
neighboring institutions. In this way, elimination of individual courses or
partial elimination of a program would not preclude the students enrolled
in one university from engaging in academic work that is of interest to
them. Such consortia efforts could also become a strong marketing device
for all the schools joined in the consortium compact.

- Initiating consortium efforts also could lead to the more radical move of
allowing public and private institutions in a state to share staff and faculties (Cohen, 1998). Sharing staff and faculty would dramatically cut back
on the amount of instructional costs for both institutions. However, it
should be noted that such a change could result in greater difficulties. For
example, determining which institution had priority when it comes to curriculum planning or providing access to students outside of class, would be
just two potential areas of tension and debate.

- Productivity and greater efficiency can also be encouraged by accelerating
graduation rates, including those based on shortened time to degree
(Cohen, 1998). For example, expanding course offerings through consortia
arrangements or the use of information technology will increase learning
and productivity and will reduce the time to degree.

- The final recommendation regarding productivity addresses the future impact
of technology. More institutions are moving toward incorporating technology as an integral part of their campus operation and as a means of increasing overall productivity (Green and Gilbert, 1995; Massy and Zemsky, 1990).
In 1996, one survey revealed that one-third of all college courses required the
use of electronic mail, one-fourth involved the use
of the Internet, and one-eighth required the use
of multimedia services (Green, 1997). According to
experts, thoughtful integration of technology into
both the instructional arena and the world of
research also may result in greater efficiency and
greater productivity. In addition, technology may
replace some of the traditional activities of faculty,
such as teaching through the lecture format, thereby

Technology may replace some of the traditional activities of faculty, such as teaching through the lecture format.

freeing up time for activities that contribute to higher level skills in students or make better use of faculty expertise (for example, designing new coursework, pedagogical research, and assessment of students). It has also been noted that as students learn at a time, place, and pace of their own choosing, their productive learning and their progress to levels of proficiency could increase. Further, technology will allow for the customization of higher education, improving its value to students and to the society being served. Finally, technology can ease the institution's problems with time and space, and will reduce the demands on facilities by slowing "the rise in costs related to adding new faculty and staff, library holdings, and buildings" (Meyer, 1998, p. 70). However, although a substantial number of institutions are committing financial resources for technology to be used in both academic and administrative adaptations, (El-Khawas, 1995; Green, 1997), technology's use in the academic classroom poses the foremost challenge. Many professors have refused to incorporate technology in their teaching strategies (Van Dusen, 1997), thus possibly eliminating vital information on what impact, if any, technology has on faculty productivity. The use of technology will also summon faculty to become more experimental concerning student learning needs, which may place them in conflict with their own preferences (research) (Plater, 1995). For an honest assessment of the impact technology may have on faculty productivity, colleges and universities should 1) establish a venue where administrators, faculty, and students can discuss and analyze technology utilization and purchases; 2) affirm the value of technology-based learning from a number of research viewpoints; and 3) tie any technology use in the classroom of teaching, learning, and research to the overall mission of the college or university (Van Dusen, 1997).

The Kent State University vignette from Wergin (1994) provides a complex scenario of how senior leadership is challenged by productivity issues that impact faculty and university objectives.

Kent State University

With more than 34,000 students on eight campuses and some twenty-five different doctoral programs, Kent State University is a large university with a complex mission. As an "emerging research university" (a term used in the mission statement), Kent State has struggled in the past few years with accommodating the changing perceptions of the importance of teaching in relation to the importance of research and the increasing demand to better balance the two.

Beginning with her 1991 inaugural address, Kent State President Carol Cartwright placed a high priority on the need to redefine scholarship and to revisit the ways in which faculty work is evaluated and rewarded. One of her first acts as president was to encourage the faculty senate to take a leadership role in this effort. With her support, the senate convened a Commission on Scholarship to examine the ideas imbedded in Boyer's famous work, "Scholarship Reconsidered." After much debate and active consultation with the academic departments and the top administration, this group, chaired by Professor Glazer (now chair of the senate), produced a set of twenty principles for the evaluation and reward of faculty scholarship. These principles called for the evaluation of faculty work to be considered "first within the context of the department's mission, and subsequently within the context of the school, college, campus, and university mission."

The agreed upon principles included these key points: (1) scholarship should include the four types outlined by Boyer (called scholarship extended at Kent): discovery, integration, application, and teaching; (2) criteria should be developed at the department level, should fully reflect the diverse roles of the faculty, and should be consistently defined, applied, and understood by other disciplines; (3) after review at all levels, the administration should support department decisions; and (4) minimum standards for good citizenship (service activities not tied directly to one's own discipline) should be established by each department and required of all faculty members.

After the principles were adopted by the senate in Fall 1992, the senate chair and the provost, Myron Henry, sent a letter to all departments and schools offering a pen forum to discuss the principles and their applications. These meetings continue to the present. About the same time the senate was developing and debating the 20 principles, the University Priorities and Budget Committee (appointed by the president and chaired by the provost) was engaged in revising the defining characteristics of the university. The resulting document entitled "Kent Institutional Characteristics"(KICS), puts some flesh on the bones of the university's 1989 mission statement and incorporates scholarship extended concepts in the description of teaching, research and creative activity, as well as out reach and community service. Although the term scholarship extended is not used, to date the KICS has been endorsed by major university standing committees, the faculty senate, and the Kent Board of Trustees.

A third activity, also initiated by President Cartwright (partially in response to statewide mandates for more documentation of faculty workloads, with a not-so-subtle message that teaching needed to be valued more highly), is an ongoing faculty productivity study. Its first phase involved an intensive analysis of the ways in which faculty members in five diverse departments and schools spend their time. Rather than respond to the usual kinds of one-shot surveys, however, selected faculty in these departments kept detailed logs. The findings were revealing. The average time spent on professional activities was 50–55 hours per week; the average number of students taught by full time faculty was 74, while the average for full professor (a subset of the group) was 77; and the amount of time spent on instruction and advising related activities was equal to time spent in public service and research combined. Findings were consistent across the five disparate units. This largely anecdotal data formed the basis for a shorter, more statistically oriented survey being implemented in a much broader sample of departments. One intended outcome of these studies is to establish overall performance profiles and presumably performance standards for a cluster of departments that share a similar scholarly culture and institutional responsibilities (for example, departments within the natural sciences could develop a set of performance standards).

All of these efforts have taken place in an environment of severe fiscal austerity. For example, state funding for fiscal year 1993 was 10 percent below fiscal year 1991 levels, and faculty merit pay was temporarily suspended. Kent is an institution with collective bargaining, and, by all accounts, 1992-93 was a difficult year, as it took 11 months to reach a three-year agreement. For a time, the negotiation produced a polarizing process. Today however, the campus feels largely satisfied with the outcome; due in part to perceived improvements in campus governance. In fact, 92 percent of the voting faculty endorsed the new agreement.

To date, the most viable work on the scholarship extended front at Kent has taken place in the Department of Biological Sciences. Using the 20 principles document as a guide, the department has developed and agreed to its own criteria for the evaluation and reward of faculty scholarship. In brief, the departmental document specifies that performance is to be evaluated according to the traditional categories of research, instruction, and service, but also specifies that the relative weighting of these categories may vary according to the individual faculty member's role in the department. Further, the department recognizes the diverse nature of scholarship—in particular the four categories of discovery, integration, application, and teaching—as integral to research, instruction and service. In addition, criteria for excellence in each of these three areas have been carefully articulated, along with examples of pertinent evidence that would indicate excellence has been achieved. Department Chair Keith Ewing explained that the department was able to get so far largely because the principles comprised a "good fit" between the suggested framework and what the department was already doing. That is to say, the Department of Biological Science prior to the advent of the commission on scholarship had been involved in a long-term effort to redefine its department mission and to develop more clearly differentiated faculty roles. Making such changes initially was difficult because of the department's disciplinary diversity and because of the physical *location of its faculty—twenty-five at the main campus and eight others spread out among regional campuses. Nonetheless, the department's disciplinary diversity and its focus on applied sciences made the new framework appealing. . . . What was unclear is whether or not the process can be credited with encouraging the faculty to work together, as teamwork already is a high priority in this department.*

As might be expected, some departments on campus are making more progress in implementing the principles, while others have done little or nothing to date. One widely held perception among the faculty is that the "scholarship extended" effort is an "attack on research." Others believe the process will "water down" the criteria for promotion and tenure. In addition, the fact that they have a new president who has an ambitious agenda and who has addressed the reward system at a time when the campus is under severe financial duress, has led to some wariness and some suspicion on the part of faculty. Nevertheless, faculty leaders seem sanguine about the prospects for constructively changing the reward system. The overall environment for incremental change is strong. However, whether a significant number of departments will take up this challenge remains unclear. Thus, some on campus feel that the administration needs to keep the heat on or even needs to turn it up a little to ensure the success of implementing a more balanced system for rewarding faculty productivity.

Kent State is one of the few institutions that have actively established explicit links between a redefinition of faculty work and rewards. To that end, Provost Henry has argued "[c]onvincing individuals within a department to think in a holistic sense is probably still best facilitated by individual rewards." However, both administrators and faculty leaders agree that these holistic links will take a while to forge. As Henry notes, one of the major barriers will involve differentials in faculty responsibilities. As the Senate Chair and Provost explains, "they have not reached a clear understanding on the technical implication of redefining the roles of faculty. That

is, faculty opinions have not yet embraced the differential assign-
ment approach which would lead to some faculty spending more
time in the classroom, and more time advising, and more time with
students. Consequently, the debate right now seems to focus on the
why faculty don't have time for research and why they are not prop-
erly rewarded because all that counts is research. To date, there just
haven't been many volunteers stepping forward to teach more . . .
Perhaps more focus on collective success and less on individual star-
dom may lead us to the academic department as the key unit."

Nonetheless, Provost Henry believes that at Kent State, "we are
discussing the need to embrace a view of faculty productivity that is
more congruent with all department responsibilities, to establish links
between individual performance and reward departmental effec-
tiveness, to determine measures for department success, and to make
the resource allocation process more open."

This is all fine in theory, according to one faculty leader, but
difficult to implement in practice. Moving from the personal to the
collective view will take a long time and will require structural
changes and reasoned strategies. Getting faculty to work on collective
issues of any sort is difficult. Difficult maybe, but Kent's Depart-
ment of Biological Sciences has shown that it is not impossible
(Wergin, 1994, pp. 18–21).

The Kent State case demonstrated the difficulty that senior level administrators and faculty have in agreeing to acceptable levels of faculty productivity especially during a period of fiscal austerity. However, their long-term
objective is to create a strategic fit between the optimal mix of faculty productivity and the allocation of limited resources. This action could lead to cost
containment through the efficient use of university resources. As confirmed
by a more recent study on faculty productivity, there are two major issues:
"1) there is a demand for accountability in higher education; and 2) in order
to gain accountability, particularly at a time when roles are changing, better
performance measures are needed" (Middaugh, 2001, p. 53).

Financial Commitment to Tenure

Tenure-track faculty members at four-year public and private institutions nationwide account for approximately 52 percent of the total population of professors (American Association of University Professors, 1998). In achieving tenure, as outlined in the 1940 Statement of Principles on Academic Freedom and Tenure by the AAUP and the American Association of Colleges, faculty members now hold potentially lifetime teaching appointments in their respective institutions (Ehrenberg, 1997). Tenured faculty members are thus able to freely pursue teaching and research activities without fear of reprisal from the administration or boards of trustees into an advanced age, because under the agreement of tenure, faculty members can only be dismissed under conditions of incompetence, moral turpitude, or financial exigencies (Tallman and Ward, 1997).

Tenure is viewed by many as an intractable barrier that prevents institutions from adjusting internal resources to conform to market demand for academic programs (Chait, 1997).

One of the major considerations for the current review of the tenure system is how it exerts a pronounced impact on the financial operations of the university (Tierney, 1998; Walters, 1997). A tenured faculty line is considered part of fixed cost in most institutions of higher education, which means that regardless of the level of enrollments and the level of available operating funds, this fixed cost must be covered first by the institution (Vandament, 1989). As a result, tenure is viewed by many as an intractable barrier that prevents institutions from adjusting internal resources to conform to market demand for academic programs (Chait, 1997). This means, for example, if academic programs are less than successful in attracting the number of students needed for enrollment projections, there may not be internal flexibility in appointments that would allow administrators to reduce program offerings—especially if it is tenured professors who hold positions in the program and will not lose their positions unless the program is discontinued or the university declares its financial exigency for closing the position(s). Furthermore, even when a program is discontinued, colleges and universities are expected to find positions for those tenured faculty members in other departments. Moreover, until recently, there was little to no opportunity to evaluate the job performance of faculty members once tenure was received. However, the call for post-tenure reviews should address concerns in this area and may become instrumental as university leadership is required to manage budgets more effectively and to justify the cost per student enrolled in various programs (Tallman and Ward, 1997).

The perceived inflexibility of the tenure system in higher education has been a point of discussion in the private sector as well. Many of the traditional large, blue chip stock corporations (such as IBM, AT&T, and Johnson & Johnson) have questioned the benefits of offering lifetime employment opportunities given the uncertainty in the marketplace and the option to trim personnel cost as a way to improve profit margins (Lipman-Blumen, 1998). Accordingly,

> *Starting in the 1980s, a series of shocks hit the economy. Heightened competition, rapid technology change, and corporate mergers led to layoffs throughout American industry. In the late 1970s and early 1980s, it was the blue-collar industrial worker—often unionized—who bore the brunt of permanent job loss. Since the late 1980s, it has been white-collar, educated workers who have experienced the sharpest increases in permanent job loss. Less-educated workers still have the highest job loss rate, but their rates have fallen since the early 1980s. Hence the gap separating the job loss rate of males with a high school education and males with a college education narrowed by more than half between the early 1980s and the mid-1990s. Companies that never experienced a major layoff at firms like IBM, Kodak, and Digital Equipment—now jettison thousands of white-collar employees (Jacoby, 1999, p. 2).*

However, the ability to reduce its workforce at will has not always ensured that a company will meet its financial objectives. In the 1990s, close to half of the Fortune 500 companies that called for layoffs did not experience higher stock prices (Epstein, 1999) nor did they experience improved financial performance (Vanderheiden, De Meuse, Bergman, and Thomas, 1994). Even so, while the business sector views employees as its most valuable asset, companies continue to use reduction in the workforce as a major strategy to improve financial performance (Piturro, 1999). "Although many companies do consider their employees to be an important asset, corporate downsizing continues unabated. Layoffs reached a ten-year high of 677,795 in 1998 and totaled 438,257 for the first seven months of 1999. . . . On the surface, this slimming down seems to make sense: Companies can rid themselves of the cumbersome bureaucracy that often bogs down decision making. Most importantly, staff cuts fall directly to the bottom line" (Piturro, 1999, p. 1).

While it is true that tenure precludes a college or university from being able to downsize at will, there are financial incentives to maintain tenure. Proponents of the tenure system argue that colleges and universities actually save funds in the long run through the retention of tenured faculty. The savings are achieved by maintaining salary levels at a relatively lower rate over a period of years (when compared to the earning opportunities in the private sector) in exchange for lifetime employment (Burgan, 1996). Some administrators feel that instructional costs would increase exponentially if tenured faculty did not settle for this tradeoff. In addition, many argue that there should not be a precipitous rush to fault the tenure system when tenure may merely be being used as a smokescreen to cover for financial deficiencies in administration, governance, and financial management (Baughman and Goldman, 1997). In addition, more data is needed by institutions on "the percentage of payroll disbursed to tenured faculty members, the projected turnover of faculty members, or the number and percentage of positions shifted from one department to the next" (Chait, 1997, B4) in order to best analyze the financial effects of tenure at their respective institutions.

There are financial incentives to maintain tenure.

Nonetheless, "with colleges scrambling to provide the new, career-oriented courses that students demand, with schools hiring presidents who have corporate backgrounds, with trustees pressing administrators to keep cost down, tenure—higher education's seemingly immutable institution—is now a target" (Chait, 1997, B4). This distrust of tenure is also compounded by the fact that corporations over the past ten-year business cycle have restructured and downsized their workforces to respond to competition and profitability pressures while higher education continues the process of guaranteed employment for faculty who achieve tenure.

Currently, many university administrators are attempting to make decisions that affect the present and will affect the future mix of tenured and nontenured faculty. Between 1975 and 1995, the proportion of full-time professors on contracts increased from 9 percent to 28 percent while the proportion of tenure track positions over the same period declined by 12 percent (Wilson, 1999). A higher mix of contract versus tenured faculty allows the administration more flexibility in terms of employment decisions (such as hiring and firing), determining salary and benefit levels, and holding faculty accountable for productivity through the period of contract renewal (O'Neill, 1998). Conversely, the increased mix of contractual faculty could work against recruiting the best and brightest candidates who gravitate toward tenure track positions (Yarmolinsky, 1996). Nonetheless, it has become clear that compromises need to be made which will maintain academic freedoms for faculty while also alleviating administrators' concerns that universities will continue to be unable to control the cost of their largest expenditure item.

The first question to ask in order to achieve such a compromise is how one could restructure "tenure to fit the accomplishments and capabilities of the individual and the projected long-term needs of the institution" (Yarmolinsky, 1996, p. 16). Some of the strategies to consider include

- Increasing options on tenure contracts that would allow the university and faculty member to negotiate a limited scope of tenure in return for more financial incentives tied to performance (Yarmolinsky, 1996).
- Strategically employing part-time and adjunct faculty without upsetting the academic integrity of the respective departments (Ehrenberg, 1997).
- Increasing the ratio of full-time non-tenure track faculty to the number of tenured faculty. Financially, colleges and universities pay less in salaries and benefits to those faculty members who are not among the tenured or tenure-track ranks (Wilson, 1999). This strategy has been faulted for creating a two-tiered system among full-time faculty; nonetheless, these appointments have become part of a popular trend in higher education institutions (Leatherman, 1999).

- Providing new faculty members the choice of tenure track positions or rolling three-year contracts at higher salaries.
- Altering annual contracts by reducing the amount of months from twelve to nine in order to alter the impact of tenure (Tierney, 1998). Such alterations could account for a 25 percent reduction in annual salary. For example,

> *At other institutions, there has been discussion about what has come to be called the x-y-z funding. The assumption is that x is equivalent to one's base salary, y is what the individual (or unit) adds on to it from outside funding, and z is what the individual currently earns or lower than what the norm has been. Thus, in a reconfigured funding formula, tenured Professor Jones last year may have earned $60,000, but this year, we will define her base (x) as $50,000 and assume that grants or extra teaching will enable Jones to achieve the additional $10,000 (y); if she receives extra income or a bonus, the money would go beyond the $60,000 (z)* (Tierney, 1998, p. 631).

- Hiring full-time and part-time faculty off the tenure track, thus providing institutions more opportunities to regulate professors' work assignments and the distribution of their time in accordance with student enrollments (Baldwin and Chronister, 2001).

There is another possibility, however, that may offer greater potential to reconcile the positive advantages of tenure and the need for greater institutional flexibility. Institutions may find it most productive and effective to adjust tenure with the accomplishments and capabilities of the individual and the projected long-term needs of the institution. Thus, each tenure contract would be negotiated at the time the individual was hired, around the locus of the tenure commitment. "The commitment could reside in a disciplinary branch or subfield, in a specific program, in an academic department, in a school, or in exceptional cases, across the college or university. The scope of tenure could be renegotiated from time to time, but only to broaden it, so that renegotiations could not be used—even directly in a punitive fashion" (Yarmolinsky, 1996, p. 16).

Summary

Under faculty compensation, instructional costs represent 32.6 percent and 26.8 percent of total expenditures at public and private four-year institutions, respectively. Along with increases in faculty salaries and the elimination of mandatory retirement, a primary concern for those charged with maintaining or reducing costs involves the increase in the average cost of fringe benefits as a percent of faculty salaries. The increase in fringe benefits costs is due primarily to rising health care costs. As a result, more scrutiny is being given to the measurement of all faculty productivity as it relates to workload and instruction. A 1993 study found that full-time tenure track salary levels were based primarily on the mix between time spent on teaching, classroom activities, research, and the number of publications. The Kent State University case exhibits how difficult it is for institutions to solve the faculty productivity problem unless it is tied to the strategic mission of the institution. Future cost drivers included in instructional expenditures could consist of an increase in the use of part-time faculty that have collective bargaining agreements (unionization).

Finally, major consideration has been given to the financial impact of the commitment to the traditional tenure system. One of the major questions is, How can tenure be restructured to accommodate the accomplishments and potential of the faculty member while meeting the long-term financial needs of the institution? One suggestion would be to increase options on tenure contracts that would allow both the university and faculty member to negotiate a limited scope of tenure in return for more financial incentives tied to performance. This strategy relates more to options presented in business models.

Are There Cost Savings
in Academic Libraries?

THE CATEGORY OF ACADEMIC SUPPORT represents approximately 7.6 percent and 6.1 percent of total expenditures from public and private four-year institutions, respectively (*The Chronicle of Higher Education Almanac,* 2001–2002). Service categories within academic support include academic administrative support, libraries, museums, and galleries to name a few, and each of these units is charged with the task of providing support services to further facilitate the mission of the institution (American Institute of Certified Public Accountants, 1994). And of these academic support units, the major cost center is the financial investment made to maintain academic libraries.

The cost of maintaining an academic library varies from one institution to the next, depending on such variables as the mission, the size of student body, and the number of faculty and other personnel. Typically, library costs include acquisitions, technical services, public service, personnel, and the cost of maintaining library buildings. During the 1970s, directors of libraries were under pressure to operate in an environment of reduced budgets, escalating labor costs, preservation issues, space problems, and an increased need to respond, in a timely manner, to requests from students and faculty for up-to-date literature along with meeting the need to acquire emerging technologies (Battin, 1982). The dual demands of reductions in budgets and of emerging or improved technologies worked to undermine the purchasing power of university libraries. These demands were compounded further in the 1980s by a reduction in federal government funding for libraries and an increase in journal subscription rates (Nauman, 1997). In the 1990s, university libraries were confronted with continual escalations in general subscription costs (which have risen well above the rate of inflation), along with increases in demand for services from internal and external users, and with escalating costs associated with incorporating new technologies into the existing library system (Wittenberg, 1996). Moreover, between 1974 and 1990, university libraries were spending more funds for materials but receiving less back, in real terms, after adjustment for inflation. For example, between the fifteen-year period from 1981 to 1995, when compared to the rate of inflation, the acquisition budgets of eighty-nine university libraries increased on average by 82 percent. However, the average library in this group lost 38 percent of its purchasing power due to double-digit inflation from acquisitions (Hawkins, 1996). In addition, actual budget allocations for many college and university libraries' operations did not conform to the 1986 guidelines suggested by the ACRL Standards for College Libraries, which called for library acquisitions that would constitute "six percent of the total institutional budget for education and general purposes. . . . The library's appropriation shall be augmented above the six percent level depending upon the extent to which [the library] bears responsibility for acquiring, processing, and servicing audiovisual materials and microcomputer resources" (*Standards for College Libraries,* 1986, p. 9).

> **Between 1974 and 1990, university libraries were spending more funds for materials but receiving less back, in real terms, after adjustment for inflation.**

During these same time periods, other areas within these institutions benefited from the libraries' reduced share of the academic budget. This is evidenced by the fact that over the last twenty years there have been major shifts in the funding allocated to other areas such as administration, research, student services, and community affairs (Goudy, 1993). To attract the best and brightest students, colleges and universities created additional administrative positions that would primarily manage state-of-the-art student services programs and facilities. At the same time, some of these institutions promoted aggressive research agendas to garner greater prestige and recognition, spending funds to attract research-oriented faculty for the respected programs. These efforts, to some extent, have worked to shift funding away from other areas within the academy, particularly academic libraries. In an effort to receive a larger share of college and university budgets, many feel that academic library departments should report directly to the chief information officer (or vice president of technology) of the university as opposed to the vice president of academic affairs (O'Donnell and Newman, 2000). Internally, academic libraries have had to contend with increasing acquisition costs, the utilization of technology, and outsourcing decisions.

Acquisition Costs

The increase in acquisition costs, in large part, has been driven by expensive high-end journal subscriptions, especially in the disciplines of science, technology, law, medicine, and business (Okerson, 1986; Rea, 1998). Journal prices have risen well above the economy's inflation rate and beyond cost increases within the journal publishing industry (Stoller, Christopherson, and Miranda, 1996). For example, an annual library subscription to the Journal of Comparative Neurology cost $1,920 in 1985; in 2000, the cost was $15,000 (English and Hardesty, 2000). Many feel that the runaway prices in this area are due to a perceived monopolistic environment and price discrimination within the publishing industry (Stoller and others, 1996). Although evidence does not clearly point to a monopoly in the journal publication industry, there are signs of price discrimination. In particular, three different types of price discrimination have been identified:

> **Many feel that the runaway prices in journal subscriptions are due to a perceived monopolistic environment and price discrimination within the publishing industry.**

1. Commercial and noncommercial journal publishers have normally charged academic libraries considerably higher prices (often three or more times as high) than they do individual subscribers for the same quantity of an identical product, that is, a one-year journal subscription (Joyce and Mertz, 1985).

2. Western European journal publishers have charged American buyers considerably higher prices than they do European subscribers for the same quantity of an identical product, after allowing for differences in shipping cost and the risk of exchange rate fluctuations (Astle and Hamaker, 1986).

3. Publishers, particularly commercial firms, have charged far higher prices for natural science and engineering journals than for journals in other fields, on a per page basis, after allowing for any differences in production and shipping costs associated with variations in the frequency of publication (Joyce and Mertz, 1985).

4. In addition, journal publishers tend to take advantage of consortia (group purchases from member libraries) by offering member libraries access to all of their publications for an additional cost above what is paid for the original service (Goodman, 2000).

Practices such as the aforementioned have made it increasingly difficult for libraries to maintain the collection of materials demanded by the research faculty and required by graduate and undergraduate students. It also is worth noting that when university libraries attempt to secure lower prices for digital material, they often are asked to agree to provisions such as the following:

1. That there be multiyear (often three) price increase guarantees to compensate for adjustments in inflation, often at a somewhat lower rate than the historical rates for print material.

2. That there be upward price adjustments for increases in content, which in most cases are capped at lower rates than are typical for print journals.

3. That the publishers be protected against declines in revenue through cancellation of service.

4. That fair-use rights typical for print journals are abrogated for digital journals' use (Whisler and Rosenblatt, 1997).

Eastern Washington University academic library experienced the problem of attempting to protect the continuation of journal subscriptions during a lean budgetary period at the expense of new book acquisitions (Rea, 1998).

This action resulted in a drop in the number of books-to-undergraduate student ratio in areas of interest important to undergraduate instruction (Rea, 1998). To reduce cost and protect against this imbalance during the next budgeting cycle, it was recommended by the dean of libraries that the new budget concentrate on three strategies:

- *the identification of a core collection of journals, indexes, and books;*
- *a formula for allocating to the departments the resource dollars not required to support the core collection; and*
- *a pilot project in direct document-delivery for faculty* (Rea, 1998, p. 145).

Additional strategies outside of the Eastern Washington University case that have been considered for cost containment in journal purchases include

1. The conviction that the need for and use of information is highly elastic as access is improved in concert with rapidly-evolving advances in electronic technology. This elasticity holds true for both print—and electronically—delivered information. Thus, in a changing arena, at best, the librarians learned they could be only partially correct in their decisions for selecting material and thus realized that the information being used was evolving and dynamic.
2. The understanding that group purchases are superior to individual purchases. Consortium purchasing enhances vendor revenues and profits while lowering the library unit cost of purchase. Many consortiums save anywhere from 20 percent to 70 percent when buying as a group as compared to the economies of the purchasing power of individual libraries.
3. The belief that the focus must be on information expansion and cost effectiveness. Rationing the acquisition of information as a cost-containment mechanism may be seen as a survival tactic but it does not constitute a strategic approach that encourages success. (Sanville, 1999, p. 50).

In addition, a study commissioned by the Association of Research Libraries (ARL) implied that professional associations create new journals as a nonprofit alternative to commercial publishers. Given additional competition from universities and professional associations entering the journal publication business, this could work to stabilize prices in the marketplace (Stoller, Christopherson, and Miranda, 1996).

Technology Impact on Academic Libraries

A constant factor in the cost mix for libraries remains the role of technology. Technology functions as an ongoing expenditure both in its use in maintaining publications and in its use in the very operations of the library system (Whisler and Rosenblatt, 1997). When attempting to integrate existing and emerging technologies into the cost structure the challenge is even more daunting for library operations. "With the advent of online catalogs, online indices, and the Internet, more students and faculty can pursue the plethora of sources which exist out there" (Schroeder, 1995, p. 1). One of the primary purposes of incorporating technology into libraries was to gain cost efficiencies in processing operations and to respond to the end users' (faculty, students, and staff) need for more information through electronic journal publications (Getz, 1997; Whisler and Rosenblatt, 1997). In the management of electronic information, libraries now are cast as active systems rather than as brick-and-mortar repositories for storing reading materials (Martin, 1998). Consequently, research is conducted not only from conventional reading material, but also by manipulating information through computer terminals. As a result, libraries have had to increase budgets to account not only for electronic information, but also for the corresponding hardware (computers, printers, software packages). Concurrently, they have had to structure their needs within the overall cost strategies of the university.

In recent years, libraries have come a long way in integrating technology and technological services into their operations and in understanding the concomitant impact such integration has made on their cost structures. When OPACs and then CD-ROMs replaced card catalogs, libraries invested in the requisite desktop computers and mainframes that were costly in terms of

> **A constant factor in the cost mix for libraries remains the role of technology.**

the initial outlay of money required to purchase them, costly in terms of the valuable floor space they occupied, and costly in terms of ongoing maintenance (Majka, 2000). Networking these systems to fit specific library needs also incurred new costs. In addition, upgrades from new CD-ROM vendors each month involved valuable staff time.

However, the current use of technology is now operating in favor of libraries. "Second-generation library systems (and data processing systems in general) have enhanced the benefits and reduced the cost of this exchange. From a library point of view, second-generation OPACs now run on client-server networks that utilize a relatively inexpensive workstation rather than a substantial mainframe to house the database. Information now is transmitted to a network of personal computers, of rapidly decreasing price coupled with increasing capabilities to utilize nearly universal and compatible network software, operating systems, and user interfaces (via WWW browsers)" (Majka, 2000, p. 70).

The strategic plans for and mission of a university or college often inform how the costs associated with academic support should be prioritized. In the case of restructuring Meriam Library at California State University, Chico, to fit the needs of technology, its goal was to 1) integrate formally independent library units, 2) ally the library and the computing center, 3) develop and implement state and regional consortia, and 4) enhance the value of the academy's contribution to society at large (Rankin, 2000). These goals supported the overall strategic plan for the university whose first priority was to create and enhance innovative, high-quality, student-centered learning environments, as the learning environments included the ongoing commitment to and maintenance of a vibrant library that provided opportunities for both learning and research (Rankin, 2000).

It also is worth noting that electronic acquisitions raise questions concerning the terms of what is being acquired, archival rights, who has access to and control of the information, what legal stipulations may apply in terms of how the acquisitions are used, and how price is determined (Davies, 1998). In an attempt to gain insight into expanding costs in the use of technology, Southern Methodist University hired consultants to help it develop and reengineer a plan for administrative and academic computing and equipment to enhance its capabilities in electronic communications and networking both on and off campus (Pastine, 1996). At this time, it could be said that the end results have left the university with more questions than answers. The university had difficulty in tracking all costs pertaining to computing, such as the costs associated with training and consulting. There also were debates concerning how the mainframe should be allocated in terms of the portion allocated to the library as opposed to that allocated to academic units. In addition, staffing costs related to computing were not well identified, as there were inconsistencies in the correct expense code used to define the work. Similar expenses for computing often

> **Planning for technology requires cooperation among parts of the university that often are considered independent of one another.**

were paid from different account codes. Meanwhile, changes in telecommunications accounts created additional problems. Overall, the lack of coordination within and among the academic libraries and other computing facilities on the SMU campus demonstrated that planning for technology requires cooperation among parts of the university that often are considered independent of one another. However, in an effort to "improve productivity and increase cooperation, collaboration, and open up new teaching and learning environments" (Pastine, 1996, p. 29) planning was initiated. And it has been suggested that the foundation for most of the suggested cost containment strategies in the use of technology in university libraries involve the formulation of a strategic plan that is linked to the university's mission, scholarship, and research needs (Hughes, Rockman, and Wilson, 2000; Martin, 1998; Pastine, 1996; Rankin, 2000). Some of the more specific strategies stipulate that

- The pricing of specialized databases should be contingent upon an expected number of uses, not total campus FTE;
- The unit cost for electronic material should be less than the print version and the library should not be forced to buy both versions;
- Unit cost should decrease as volume of use increases; and
- The cost of providing access services and the cost of material should be separate (Dwyer, 1999).

To prepare practical budgets that meet the specific needs of their constituencies, there must be an ongoing dialogue between librarians and the faculty and students (Hughes, Rockman, and Wilson, 2000). There also should be a clear understanding about those concerns that affect costs and those that affect service (Kantor, 1985). In addition, university libraries should take advantage of collaboration and partnerships. For example, the Journal STORrage project developed through the Andrew W. Mellon Foundation was designed to aid non-profit organizations in gaining access to scholarly material at a cost savings to participants (Guthrie, 1997). The cost of this project is based on six categories:

1. Production—work performed by scanning subcontractors;
2. Conversion—input of index information;
3. Storage and access—preserving the database at various locations;
4. Software development—maximizing the usefulness of data as technology changes;
5. User support—providing help-desk services;
6. Administration and oversight—effective managment and control of operations (Guthrie, 1997).

Similarly, the Johns Hopkins University Press and the Milton S. Eisenhower Library at the Johns Hopkins University developed an opportunity (Project MUSE) for network-based access to scholarly journals in the areas of humanities, social sciences, and mathematics (Neal, 1997). "Funded initially by grants from The Mellon Foundation and The National Endowment for the Humanities, Project MUSE seeks to create a successful model for electronic scholarly publishing characterized by affordability and wide availability" (Neal, 1997, p. 250). The expected outcomes in the use of this technology are based on cost reductions, gains in productivity, increased access for the user, and convenience. The Stevens Institute of Technology case from The Council for Library and Information Resources (1999), revealed a significant paradigm shift that aligned university needs with the reality of cost constraints for its library.

Stevens Institute of Technology

Electronic Access, Not Subscriptions http://www.lib.stevens-tech.edu/ index.html.

Stevens Institute of Technology is an urban university located in a park-like setting in Hoboken, New Jersey, across from midtown Manhattan. Stevens offers baccalaureates, master's, and doctoral degrees in engineering, science, computer science, and management, as well as baccalaureate degrees in the humanities and liberal arts. It enrolls some 1,400 undergraduates and 2,000 graduate students, who are taught by 102 full-time faculty. The institutional budget is $65 million, of which about $823,000 goes for library operation. There are five librarians and four support staff. Together with graduate student assistants, they provide services to Stevens's students and faculty.

Stevens has a reputation for innovation and leadership in the use of computers in engineering. It was one of the first campuses in the country to be fully networked, to require that all entering students have personal computers (1983), and to offer online searching to all faculty and students as a fee-based service.

In 1991, at the direction of the Board, the university administration imposed an austerity program that included a reduction of $250,000 from the library's budget. That amount was equivalent to what the library was paying for its journal subscriptions. Library Director Richard Widdicombe and his staff, encouraged by the president and supported by the faculty, decided that only a radical new means of delivering information would allow the library to continue supporting teaching and research. As a result, it was agreed that the library would drop all research-oriented periodicals and supply the information by acquiring more electronic media and buying documents. (The library still subscribes to some 150 general-interest magazines.) This change was made possible in part due to the fact that there is a network-connected computer on the desk of every faculty member and student; thus it became possible *to experiment with a new way of delivering journal articles to the Stevens community.*

The decision to rely completely on electronic access was controversial, as it was in pre-World Wide Web days. But the decision was preceded by more than fifteen years of research and experimentation, was inspired by curiosity about what research tools were being used, and, was fueled by the budgetary limitations on subscriptions. The periodical list had long held up to rigorous scrutiny, and the college had been winnowing its subscriptions for some time. Beginning with some 1,555 titles, the list was narrowed down to just over 500 by the time the decision was made to drop paper-based research periodicals.

In its efforts to cull periodicals, the library had employed several strategies to identify the most effective core of print materials for supporting chemistry, physics, mathematics, and the engineering curriculum. It used the database and hardware of the Philadelphia-based Institute for Scientific Information (ISI) to compare ISI's Science Citation Index cited in Stevens's journals. Titles were ranked by the frequency of "hits." The journals that were not cited and those that were used infrequently at Stevens were eliminated. Subsequent efforts to eliminate less-unused journals included asking faculty for candidates for weeding and affixing cards to periodicals urging browsers to mark each use. Combined circulating and browsing statistics were compared with those of other libraries that support engineering programs, to learn which journals had the highest use by students and faculty. The experiment revealed that the use of periodicals is quite specific to an institution and that most journals in an engineering college become dated only a year or two after publication. The library staff also surveyed publications authored by Stevens's faculty for source citations. They found that a wide variety of sources were cited, but no identifiable core of journals.

During the process of trying to assemble the best collection of periodicals for its purpose, new notions of library service began to surface. The decision to switch to the new system made by the library director, was based on the following findings:

- *The data collected over fifteen years showed that the library's clientele had very specific needs and would not care where the information came from.*
- *Stevens Institute, with its emphasis on technical training and practical research, did not need the broad categories of information traditionally associated with liberal education. Moreover, the budget would never allow the purchase of sufficient resources—books or journals—to meet all the needs of Stevens's faculty and students.*
- *With the advent of searchable electronic databases, those libraries able to identify specific specialized information needs of their clientele could be at the forefront of a paradigm shift in which quick access to information would be more important than owning it.*

Under the new system, research processes have been expedited. Students and faculty can look quickly at full-text articles. Students create electronic bibliographies, check the full text, and then rework their research path, moving forward in the same or new directions. The library has had to make trade-offs in order to provide electronic resources. Fewer people come to the library and the librarians miss the contact with students and faculty, but they are aware of similar trends elsewhere as more libraries offer more electronic services. The number of books in the library is growing incrementally and back issues of journals are gone; consequently, space is less of a problem and the library staff plans to establish clusters of workstations in the freed-up spaces. Dropping research journals suggests large cost savings, but some of the savings in subscription costs were lost to subsequent budget reductions. On the other hand, dealing with cutbacks made cost transfers easier to accomplish. As the numbers balance out, budget lines for journals and mono-

graphs fell sharply, but since 1991, costs associated with electronic resources have risen, as have expenditures for personnel. (Council for Library and Information Resources, 1999, pp. 64–66).

Outsourcing in Academic Libraries

Administrators have also touted outsourcing in academic libraries as a possible cost containment option, but the concept has been received with caution by library directors (Hill, 1998; Nuzzo, 1999; Osif and Harwood, 2000). By definition, outsourcing in academic libraries is supposed to produce cost effectiveness within the operation by contracting out services for such specialized tasks as system design, translation, and large-scale microfilming (White, 2000). In addition, private contractors have also been used to reduce backlogs and handle routine operations such as processing book orders. The generally agreed upon goal of outsourcing library operations (as it is in the business private sector) is to increase productivity while reducing overall costs (Abel-Kops, 2000). With the dawn of the new century, academic library administrators are faced with the challenge from their user base of providing increased access to information (in both printed and electronic forms), but doing so in the context of tightened budgets and aggressive competition from the nonacademic, for-profit world (Abel-Kops, 2000).

The generally agreed upon goal of outsourcing library operations is to increase productivity while reducing overall costs.

Since the early 1990s, concern for academic libraries has switched from whether to implement outsourcing to deciding which services would be the best candidates for outsourcing. For example, some libraries have outsourced the cataloging operation—one of the most vital and longstanding functions of any library—for years (Hill, 1998). The process has been expensive because of the use of highly trained staff. In addition, the process is so time-consuming that many libraries would be unable to complete other tasks (Hill, 1998). This type of outsourcing has worked because the needs were obvious and there was no loss in staff or control of the library operation in seeking an alternative service provider to do the work.

Nevertheless, many library directors dispute the effectiveness of using outsourcing and feel that cost effectiveness can be achieved without the use of private sector contractors (Nuzzo, 1999; Schneider, 1998; Schuman, 1998). Their argument against outsourcing also includes intangibles such as the quality of the service being provided and upholding the dignity of the profession, which should be factored into cost considerations and work decisions (Nuzzo, 1999). A survey on catalog outsourcing at academic libraries conducted in the late 1990s found that outsourcing was not a significant trend among academic libraries (Libby and Caudle, 1997). However, the study also found that larger academic libraries were more likely to outsource as the size and number of titles to catalog increased yearly.

Another common outsourcing job involves photocopying. The advantages found in outsourcing photocopying involve

- Releases the library of purchasing and supporting copier operations,
- Allowing the library to concentrate on that which it does best with little diversion of library resources,
- Acquiring the use of equipment (other than photocopiers) it would not have been able to afford to provide for patrons otherwise,
- Becoming more flexible in responding to patrons' special needs (Wittorf, 1998).

Baruck College (Duchin, 1998) determined the real cost savings through outsourcing while understanding the issues associated with contracting out services that are normally performed by university employees.

Newman Library, Baruch College/CUNY

A number of factors contributed to the decision to outsource at the City University of New York (CUNY)—the need for faster cataloging, for better databases coupled with a shortage of cataloging and acquisition librarians—prompted the university to look at outside sources for what traditionally had been internal functions. Finally, the fact that the City University of New York Board of Trustees, implementing a resolution calling for the University to establish a "systems-wide library processing service," made outsourcing not only a possibility but a necessity. The goal of the trustees' resolution was to achieve substantial cost savings through consolidating acquisitions and catalog processing into a single unit, reducing staff engaged in technical services, and negotiating increased discounts with vendors. Once informed of the trustees' resolution, the librarians realized that they could follow the letter of the resolution and resolutely close down all technical services departments (including cataloging, acquisitions, serials, binding, interlibrary loan, and periodical check-in) or they could reexamine their internal policies.

Initially the librarians considered what was logical and cost effective at a local level. Then they inventoried their current practices and needs and called in consultants to review their situation and comment on possible scenarios. After these initial consultations, they determined that one of the primary objectives should be to reduce personnel costs. As a result of their decision, a number of technical service personnel re-deployed themselves to other areas. Consequently, Baruch College, one of the senior colleges of CUNY, was able to reduce technical-services staff at Newman Library from about 12 staff members to about six, without centralizing, within a few months.

From the outset, discussions about outsourcing raised a number of fears concerning whether or not individuals would lose their jobs or whether or not an "out-of-house" vendor could provide the same quality of service as an in-house vendor. Basically, the outsourcing proposal followed a standard make-or-buy situation, driven primarily by economic concerns; nonetheless, the proposal also reflected the program's objectives. The objective was concerned with ensuring cataloging quality equal to, or superior to, what they currently enjoyed. During the outsourcing process, they learned the importance of asking the vendor how to achieve this low-cost, high quality service and still make a profit. They also recognized the importance of providing for a test period in providing the service.

[The library] learned that outsourcing was not new, even for them. The fact that they use centralized online public cataloging for all 19 colleges; that they use Library of Congress resources files and OCLC; and that they use a single periodical vendor for all of CUNY all are testimony to that fact. What had created problems for the librarians was the fact that while the solution(s) were internal, the decision had not been internal. It had come from the trustees, and thus was a top-down mandate. There also was the problem of limited communication with the library community about what was happening. Nonetheless, two years into the outsource operation, Duchin, the librarian administrator, predicts that the library will cut costs for copy cataloging in half. He also noted that the library would cut the cost of original cataloging, once that is outsourced. And he discovered that a secondary benefit of outsourcing lies in the redeployment of staff to areas that require in-house coverage. Duchin reiterated that "while there is a great deal of fear and anger to be dealt with—fear of losing jobs, anger at losing control, there can also be major long-range benefits to the library" (Duchin, 1998, pp. 111–115).

As this vignette demonstrated, one of the means of ensuring that the process of outsourcing works is to initiate a dialogue at the outset—in this case between the trustees and the librarians—and to maintain communication throughout the outsourcing process in order to alleviate fears and to ensure that the outsourcing is indeed delivering a quality product while containing costs.

Summary

Academic libraries are one of the major cost centers within the category of academic support. Library costs include acquisitions of reading material, technical services, public service, personnel, and the cost of maintaining the facilities. In the 1970s, senior-level administrators in charge of library services were under pressure to operate normally despite reduced budgets, escalating labor costs, preservation issues, space problems, and the need to respond to changing technology. These pressures were compounded further in the 1980s when federal funding for academic libraries was reduced. In the 1990s, library budgets were hard-pressed to keep pace due to reallocations of funding to other areas such as student services, research, and administration positions.

Within the operation of academic libraries, the increase in acquisition costs (driven in large part by expensive high-end journal subscriptions), has forced library directors to be more creative in covering rising expenses. For example, in the Eastern Washington University case, group purchases of journals were superior to individual purchases because consortium purchasing enhances vendor revenues and profits while lowering the library unit cost of purchase. When integrating existing and emerging technologies into the cost structure, the challenge is even more daunting for library operations. Academic libraries have had to increase budgets to account not only for electronic information, but also for the corresponding hardware such as computers, printers, and software packages.

It is worth noting, however, that in recent years the use of technology is shifting in favor of the academic library as a result of the development of less expensive workstations. In addition, administrators have touted outsourcing for such specialized tasks as system design and large-scale microfilming as a possible cost containment option through contracting out services. However, some library directors dispute the effectiveness of using outsourcing and feel that cost effectiveness can be achieved without the use of private sector contractors. A study conducted in 1997 confirmed that outsourcing was not a significant trend among academic libraries, but also concluded that larger academic libraries were more likely to outsource as the size and number of titles increased annually. The supporting cases point to those institutions that do engage in outsourcing to fully understand how the process will contribute to cost savings, necessitate the redeployment of staff, and develop lines of communication that will ensure the success of any outsourcing endeavors.

> **It is worth noting that in recent years the use of technology is shifting in favor of the academic library as a result of the development of less expensive workstations.**

Can Plant Operations and Facilities Continue to Be Ignored?

PLANT OPERATION EXPENDITURES represent 6.6 percent and 6.1 percent respectively of total expenditures in public and private four-year institutions (*Chronicle of Higher Education Almanac,* 2001). Plant operations include expenditures associated with services and maintenance of grounds and facilities, as well as all cost associated with utilities (heat, water, and electricity), fire protection, property insurance and similar items (American Institute of Certified Public Accountants, 1994). Initially, this expenditure was viewed as having an indirect relationship to the central mission of the institution. For example, during the fiscal crises of the 1980s, as a general rule, university administrators sacrificed the upkeep of facilities (including maintenance of boilers, roofs, and equipment), in order to re-allocate resources to academic programs that were in danger of shutting down (Flanagan, 1991). Consequently, colleges and universities neglected critical upkeep in plant operations and facilities in an effort to realize short-term cost savings. However, it later became clear that the decisions to delay upkeep also delayed the conscious planning necessary to determine strategic direction of the academy (Hatzia, 1998; Huish and Pieter, 1998; Schaeffner, 1996; Yeoman, Palani and McKee, 1998). This made the situation even worse.

> *America's colleges and universities' facilities are decaying. The "time bomb," as many have called it, continues to tick. At risk is the ability of colleges and universities to fulfill their mission to teach and research in an increasingly knowledge-based society. The issue is much broader than life and safety. Aging and deteriorating*

facilities pose a threat to the first class learning and the advanced research required by America in the coming decades. Like much of this country's infrastructure of highways, bridges, and transportation facilities, higher education has suffered from chronic under-investment in capital renewal and replacement. Some experts believe that the "bomb" may have already detonated (Rush and Johnson, 1989, p. 4).

Deferred Maintenance

Deferred maintenance is defined as "work that has been deferred on a planned or unplanned basis due to lack of funds in an annual budget cycle" (Rose, 1999, p. 16). Further, deferred maintenance "is the term commonly applied to larger or more expensive maintenance work that can be delayed and is not performed when needed or reported, usually because its cost is beyond the annual maintenance and operating budget of the physical plant department" (Suber, 1982, p. 12). It was estimated in 1995 that it would take roughly $26 billion to eliminate the accumulated deferred maintenance in colleges and universities (Reindl, 1998). Of the $26 billion, $5.7 billion or 22 percent is of the amount budgeted deemed to be urgent (those repairs that must be performed in an effort to maintain safety). In addition, according to some scholars in the field, these figures may be conservative, as they do not address infrastructure costs that could add 20 to 25 percent more to the overall deferred maintenance backlog (Kaiser, 1993).

The genesis of why maintenance has been deferred at colleges and universities can be traced back to the late 1950s. Because there was an expectation of increased enrollment of new students (primarily from the ranks of former military personnel who financed their education with the federal government's GI Bill), colleges and universities needed to expand their numbers of buildings (Suber, 1982). The advent of the Civil Rights movement in the 1960s and 1970s, when traditional majority institutions began admitting minority students, also led to increased enrollments and the need for campus expansion. During this time the benefits of a college education were widely believed in, and as a result, American society held education funding as a top priority. Such beliefs produced increased enrollments from 2.7 million in the 1950s to 12.5 million in 1990, a 400 percent increase (Rush, 1991). In addition, from 1950 to 1990, the number of colleges and universities grew from 1,800 to 3,300.

The conflict between devoting funds either to expansion or to upkeep of the facilities created deferred maintenance backlogs that now have become one of the major issues facing higher education institutions (Hackett and Morgan, 1996). The common practice of dedicating resources to expansion while deferring maintenance during the building boom years of the seventies compounded the problem for universities in the eighties and nineties (Suber, 1982). The issue of maintaining buildings was further complicated by the imposition of regulatory standards, mandated by state and federal governments, that included requests for asbestos removal as well as request for renovations to make buildings handicap accessible (Rush, 1994).

It has been estimated that public institutions carry a higher burden of deferred maintenance than do private institutions. This is primarily because public institutions "1) have the highest ratio of deferred maintenance to facility replacement value and one of the lowest spending rates on deferred maintenance, 2) spending on operation and maintenance of physical plant has declined over the past decade after adjustments for inflation, and 3) have more square feet currently in construction than in renovation" (Reindl, 1998, p. 11). Nonetheless, costs could range from $30 million to as high as $100 million per institution in both categories (Kaiser, 1993). This means, quite simply, that college and university capital budgets would have to be increased by these amounts in an effort to upgrade their facilities.

Overall, colleges and universities have neglected the buildup of deferred maintenance costs. Such neglect, coupled with fewer constant dollars being allocated to capital assets, compounds the funding problem that institutions of higher learning confront. Moreover, deferred maintenance costs do not even begin to address the impact of the cost of technology; for example, technological equipment and facilities for distance education that impact teaching and student services need to be accounted for as well (Kaiser, 1993).

Some of the recommendations in contending with deferred maintenance, from a cost containment perspective, include

- Approving an increase in overall funding for capital budgets that includes funds to draw down current deferred maintenance accounts to zero (Illinois Board of Higher Education, 1997; Texas Higher Education Coordinating Board, 1995).
- Providing an annual facilities audit. "The facilities audit systematically and routinely identifies facility deficiencies and functional performance of campus facilities through an inspection program and observation reports. The audit process helps maintenance management and the institution's decision makers recommend actions for major maintenance and capital renewal" (Kaiser, 1993, p. 1).
- The incorporation of a facilities and replacement program.

    A systematic and cost effective approach to planning and budgeting that extends the life and retains the useable condition of facilities and system, not normally covered in the annual operations budget, including but not limited to the following:

    1. *Deferred maintenance;*
    2. *Capital renewal and replacement;*
    3. *Facilities remodeling and renovation for functional improvements;*
    4. *Retrofitting for energy conservation;*
    5. *Elimination of health and life safety problems;*
    6. *Provisions for accessibility for persons with disabilities; and*
    7. *Compliance with federal, state, and local regulatory requirements* (Kaiser, 1993, p. 5).

- Funding a facility and maintenance plan at a two-percent level of annual budget (Flanagan, 1991). This would dramatically increase average allocation and create a level of financial commitment annually from the institution.
- Requiring a specific amount set aside for repair and replacement of the physical plant at a specific replacement value percentage. Also, requiring the submission of a deferred maintenance plan or survey outlining the

condition or work needed (South Carolina Commission on Higher Education, 1992; Suber, 1982).

- Undertaking strategic facility planning to prioritize needs (Kaiser, 1993). A strategic planning process would provide a critical review of how the facility and plant operation is contributing to the mission of the institution and would concurrently identify internal and external issues that could affect cost containment opportunities.
- Delaying or canceling new construction (Kaiser, 1993). This could provide additional operating funds to reduce accumulated deferred maintenance backlogs while forcing the college or university to focus on reinforcing the current infrastructure prior to considering new costly construction.
- Raising funds for maintenance through endowments for new buildings (Kaiser, 1993). This would establish an ongoing fund to accompany the construction of new buildings to prevent maintenance backlogs.
- Managing the facilities' portfolio (facility assets) with a common set of goals and objectives as to how the endowments are managed. This would include

1. Establishing critical baseline data about facility conditions through a detailed, structure inspection process.
2. Estimating short- and long-term renewal needs utilizing the data obtained from the facility inspection.
3. Creating decision-support models to calculate alternative reinvestment rates and the impact those rates have on short- and long-term facility conditions.
4. Reporting on the facilities portfolio to government boards, senior administrative management, and managers responsible for maintaining the portfolio (Rush, 1991).

- Evaluating the total cost of each project before decisions are made. Such an evaluation should include estimating long-term and short-term maintenance needs through a careful inspection of the facility. Those needs should be calculated by taking into account investment rates and the university's endowment and portfolio management (Rush, 1991). In addition, when evaluating the total cost of a profit, the projected life expectancy of rehabilitated buildings should be analyzed in relation to the costs that would be incurred by building a new structure (Fickes, 1999; Grimm, 1986; Schaeffer, 1999).

The University of Scranton points to the establishment of a facilities plan that helped to control deferred maintenance issues.

University of Scranton
In the late 1970s, the University of Scranton developed and implemented a five-year facilities, maintenance, and improvement program that would control the problems associated with deferring maintenance. The university also developed an annual facilities maintenance plan (FMP) for annual plant repair and maintenance items. The FMP included ordinary building repairs and maintenance to preserve existing facilities in a serviceable condition and to prevent the build up of deferred maintenance. In addition, the university developed a facilities improvement plan (FIP) for projects that would be financed through the capital budget. These projects consisted of efforts to renovate or modify existing facilities, efforts to build new facilities, and efforts that involved space renovations and support for grants.

The university also produced a three-year list of potential deferred maintenance projects. These coordinated plans of action were developed to support the goal of academic excellence and to enhance the institution's ability to continue to attract and retain students by maintaining a functional, safe, and attractive campus.

As cited in Flanagan (1991),

> *As a result of persistent and aggressive plans, the University of Scranton technically had no deferred maintenance backlog. The University developed a schedule of potential ongoing preventive maintenance projects covering a three-year period. This schedule also enabled them to avoid a buildup of actual deferred maintenance due to the requirement that the university maintain a forward-looking repair and maintenance program. Moreover, in order to maintain existing facilities in a serviceable condition and*

to keep deferred maintenance under control, the school funded the FMP at a level of 2 percent of the annual budget. An important element of the University of Scranton plan that distinguished it from many other preventive maintenance programs is that, from the outset, it included adequate staffing, compensation, organization and management of the program.

The key elements of the University of Scranton plan involved the long-range goal of professionalizing the campus facility management team. According to the University's plan of action such professionalism involved developing a proper organization with positions staffed by qualified persons, emphasizing managerial skills, to carry out goals and objectives of campus programs. Professionalism on the Scranton campus involves the following activities:

- *Establishing correct missions and functions;*
- *Establishing the proper balance of job descriptions (professionals, managers, tradespeople, mechanics, etc.);*
- *Automating systems and processes, such as work orders, computer assisted design, and facility management programs;*
- *Developing performance and productive standards;*
- *Developing experience ratios for funding and cost estimates* (Flanagan, 1991, pp. 10, 12).

Outsourcing

While plant operations managers have been forced to focus on the maintenance needs of the physical plant, it is also important for them to recognize the impact of the various services that fall under the purview of plant operations, from creating a safe learning environment for students to overseeing the electrical needs of the entire campus. Outsourcing has become a vital means of providing many of these services and of being cost efficient in doing so. Outsourcing, which is the contracting out of university services to an outside vendor, gained greater and greater recognition as an efficient means of containing costs. Even most private industry companies have experienced benefits from the reduction in and control of costs achieved through outsourcing (Figg, 2000).

A significant segment of colleges and universities in the United States provide various services for students and faculty that are outsourced, and the interest in and use of private businesses to outsource is growing (Wertz, 1997). The primary reasons for the growth in outsourcing are the opportunity to increase quality of service, the utilization of the latest technology, the opportunity to contain costs, and the ability to secure other sources of revenue (Wertz, 1997). Initially, outsourcing primarily involved seeking external vendors for food service and bookstores, but currently outsourcing extends to other departments within the academy (Kaganoff, 1998). For example, some institutions are contracting out services for remedial education programs (Gose, 1998). Other institutions are using outsourcing as a means of becoming more creative with their student housing by establishing partnerships with private real-estate developers. What has emerged from such partnerships is state-of-the-art housing facilities and expanded services for students that provide an economic return for the respective private businesses while also supporting the mission of the institutions (Johannesen, 1999). Many colleges and universities have also discovered that revenue from this venture can be plowed back into the institution to reduce cost in other areas.

Despite that the practice of outsourcing has become more prominent, several arguments have been framed for and against the use of outsourcing for facility and plant operation at colleges and universities. The benefits are 1) access to the latest equipment and technology whose cost is carried by the contractor; 2) complete control of a project that includes an agreed-upon completion date and an assurance of quality performance; 3) the ability of the administrators to devote time to other responsibilities and duties; 4) the opportunity for the academy to take advantage of economies of scale through the vendor, consequently providing the services at a lower cost; and 5) encouraging a productive atmosphere of competition among staff who traditionally have provided the particular service (Kaganoff, 1998).

Arguments against outsourcing highlight 1) the possible inability of the current university staff to manage the vendors contract because of the remote location of the project or lack of expertise by the staff in the area; 2) missed opportunities in the actual contract negotiations that would have been advantageous for the university; 3) difficulty in controlling the consistency and the quality of the work performed if more than one vendor is contracted for the same service; 4) difficulty in understanding and adjusting to the culture of the university environment on the part of the vendor, thus affecting the level and quality of service (Biddison and Hier, 1998); 5) the potential for negative impact on staff morale as a result of fear of job loss to outside vendors who perform the same functions at lower costs (Rush, 1994); 6) the possible loss of authority in dealing with services (Wertz, 1997); and 7) the potential for an unwanted external presence on campus and a negative impact on collegiality (Wertz, 1997).

When deciding whether to engage in outsourcing, an institution should evaluate all management and operating approaches from various alternatives. This suggests a "thorough understanding the campus functional area in terms of its strengths and weaknesses, challenges and opportunities, and met and unmet needs of its customers. Only then can an informed choice be made about privatizing or self-operating a campus service" (Rush, 1994, p. viii).

In addition to answering critical questions prior to making outsourcing decisions in facility and plant operations, one must arrive at an agreement that is amenable to both parties and that takes into account the affect of outsourcing on employees (Figg, 2000). In making their decisions, colleges and universities also should look to the experience of plant operation because it is a department that has long experimented with outsourcing opportunities. Various outsourcing services used by plant operations include "planning and design, project management, custodial services, and maintenance rounds" (Rush, 1994, p. ix). In determining which alternative to choose (for example, self-operation versus contracting) to achieve cost efficiency, the facility's directors should first determine if the current staff has the requisite skills to analyze whether benefits are to be garnered from new construction projects and maintenance programs and if there is an ideal symmetry between quality and the cost of administering the project (Goldstein, Kempner, and Rush, 1994). In determining whether to outsource or self-operate, some administrators discovered that both practices may benefit the institution (Getz, Gullette, Kilpatrick, and Siegfried, 1994). For example, highly technical work, such as heating and ventilation repair, may be contracted out while work in housekeeping and grounds upkeep remains self-operational (Getz and others, 1994). The more technical work can be controlled with the assurance of experts engaged at a contracted price, while a permanent staff can handle everyday tasks. Vignettes from Kaganoff (1998) in facility and plant operation highlight the experiences and issues associated with outsourcing at three institutions.

University of Pennsylvania

In an effort to save money on facilities management, the University of Pennsylvania hired a real-estate management company to manage both its on and off-campus facilities. The contract will cost Penn $5.25 million per year for ten years, but the company, in turn, also will be making two payments to Penn (a one-time payment of $26 million and a deferred payment of $6 million) because Penn is helping then outsourcing agent to establish a new subsidiary in Philadelphia. Through this outsourcing of support services, the university hopes to save as much as 15 percent of its $100 million facility budget. In order to protect some of the 175 Penn staff currently employed by facilities, the new Management Company agreed to interview and hire a specific number of Penn employees (70 percent according to the contract), of the remaining 30 percent, some staff may retire and others will be laid off. However, the facilities staff did not want their work to be outsourced and filed a class action lawsuit against the university. (Nicklin, 1997; Haworth, 1997, in Kaganoff, 1998, p. 16).

Tufts University

Tufts first outsourced its custodial work in 1974. Officials from the university defended the move by arguing that it freed up their time and energy to focus on the main purpose of the institution's teaching and research. Seventy workers switched from the campus payroll to becoming employees of the outsourced company. The original contract expired during the summer of 1997 at which point Tufts selected a new company to contract with. Again, employees were offered the chance to become employees of the new firm, but this meant the switch involved a cut in pay. As a result, the affected workers have engaged in protest and pickets, with faculty and students joining the cause (Nicklin, 1997, in Kaganoff, 1998, p. 16).

Stanford University
In order to reduce the size of its facility operations, Stanford University began to contract out more facility services. The university cut its own staff of forty and rehired a smaller number of staff. The smaller staff was made responsible for managing several contracts with the companies that took over the facilities work. The decision to outsource was promoted by complaints about the current institution's original staff taking too long and going over budget in their work (Nicklin, 1997, in Kaganoff, 1998, p. 17).

Energy Management

Energy conservation in the United States became prominent in the 1970s during the Arab oil embargo crisis (Giffin, 1990). "The 1980s taught every inhabitant of the planet not only the importance of energy in our daily lives, but also its relationship to political and economic factors" (Simko, 1990, p. 12). Since then, businesses, governments, institutions, and private households have learned to be more efficient in their use of energy in order to achieve some sort of cost savings for the user. As a result, various energy management and conservation programs (EMC) have been in place since the mid-1980s in an effort to reduce the operational costs of both commercial and institutional buildings (Karkia, 1997).

Each year, colleges and universities spend millions of dollars on electricity, natural gas, fuel oil, purchased steam, and other miscellaneous energy sources.

Each year, colleges and universities spend millions of dollars on electricity, natural gas, fuel oil, purchased steam, and other miscellaneous energy sources. In analyzing the cost distribution of a utility operation at most institutions, electric costs account for more than half the cost, fuel costs are approximately 25 percent, and the balance is consumed by renewal and replacement, deferred maintenance, labor and benefits, administration, security and insurance, supplies and material, maintenance, and water and sewer costs (Schubbe, 1999). In the aggregate, the electric power bill has been the second largest operating expense next to faculty and staff salaries for the majority of colleges and universities (Matteson, 1995). To respond to conservation in this area, the Environmental Protection Agency (EPA) developed the Green Lights voluntary membership program. This program urges colleges and universities to take advantage of energy efficient lighting upgrades on campus when and where economically feasible.

Because electricity represents a dominant role in college and university cost structures, a great deal of attention has been given to the role that the deregulation of the electric utility industry will play in influencing these costs in institutions (Larger and Klinger, 1998; Qayoumi, 1999; Schaeffer, 1999). Projected savings on electric bills for businesses and institutions under electric deregulation were first viewed to be as high as 20 percent. A more realistic number is between 5 to 15 percent (Schaeffer, 1999).

Both the electric utility deregulation and the new market will also effect the energy operations at colleges and universities. The Energy Policy Act of 1992 and the Transmission Open Access Rules of the Federal Energy Regulation Commission (FERC) determined that there need not be a business connection between ownership and the use of the electronic transmission infrastructure (Brown, 1998). The business compositions of the approximately 3,300 electric utility companies in the United States include traditional public power companies, along with the investor-owned electric companies, cooperatives, and municipalities (Qayoumi, 1999). States will have complete autonomy in establishing policy for their respective utility markets. Based on what was produced by the breakup of AT&T in the 1980s, this allows the entrance of additional companies in the utility marketplace that will compete for services, which should, in turn, produce cost savings for consumers. From conducting business solely with one entity (for example, public gas and the electric company) facility managers now will have an option in choosing the electric utility company or supplier that will be the more cost effective in generating enough electricity to service campus needs. Currently the "purveyors of electrical energy to colleges and universities are regulated utilities, independent power producers, federal producers, and on-site cogeneration facilities"; however, the "intent of deregulation is to foster increased competition between these providers, making them true 'retail' suppliers" (Matteson, 1995, p. 38).

It may be the case that this change to deregulate utility companies will not result in an easy transition for both institutions and private industry because of the lack of knowledge regarding how the marketplace for deregulated electricity will operate. During the transitional period, the areas of major concern are market structure, market power, public policy issues, and stranded cost recovery (Brown, 1998). Stranded cost is defined by the Department of Energy as costs that were incurred by utilities to serve their customers but cannot be recovered if the consumers choose other electricity suppliers (U.S. Department of Energy, 1996). In an effort to do comparative shopping on the new open market, facility managers at colleges and universities will need to have substantial knowledge of not only the types of suppliers, but also how the often volatile market works in their respective areas of the country, the different laws and regulations that govern the area, and how to negotiate contracts and provide adequate staff development (Matasek, 1999). Decisions will also have to be made concerning whether to purchase or upgrade university-owned and operated power, and generation substations, whether to investigate cogeneration options, and whether to establish partnerships with utility companies or to continue to depend on traditional methods (Matteson, 1995; McIntyre, 1995). In considering third-party ownership agreements for the operation of the power plant, colleges and universities have the same options as businesses do in determining how best to treat the asset in an effort to maximize return on investment. Because of the uncertainty of the marketplace under electricity deregulation, institutional power plants can be leased to third-party operators who have expertise in the technology, are better able to handle price fluctuations, or have the ability to better utilize personnel (Schaeffer, 1999). Being cognizant of the effects of such variables may afford institutions the opportunity to realize cost savings during a period of changes in the energy deregulation environment.

In choosing a utility supplier, one of the initial technical questions that should be addressed involves whether facility managers have adequate data regarding the campus electric load profile on an hourly, daily, and seasonal basis (Qayoumi, 1999; Schaeffer, 1999). Naturally, electric load requirements vary during the academic and nonacademic year as a result of the level of campus activities. Much of this information can be gained through the strategic placement of meters or sub meters that track the use of energy at key locations of consumption. Some of the major reasons for sub metering involve "1) determining the cost of individual facilities objectively rather than by pro-rata allocations; 2) accounting for entry costs by every department or college; 3) monitoring the efficiency of large equipment such as chillers, boilers, and compressors; 4) providing valuable data for evaluating energy conservation projects; 5) identifying performance problems and guiding preventive maintenance; and most importantly; 6) verifying savings from energy conservation projects" (Qayoumi, 1999, p. 34).

It also has been suggested that in order for facility managers to holistically quantify utility expenditures and recognize other financial and political implications as they relate to the mission of the institution, there should be a master utility plan. This plan would include 1) an assessment of the condition of the facility (plant capacity, equipment, needed improvements), 2) the documentation of facility performance (including methods for cost recovery and profiles of usage as well as projecting future capacity and consumption requirement), 3) evaluating operating policies and procedures (for example, fuel selections and budget policies), 4) an overview of the organizational environment the system operates in (impact from institutional governing boards), and 5) internal options including alternative ownership and management structures (Schubbe, 1999).

The fourth option of understanding the university environment can be critical during budget development periods. It is clear that to realize any savings in the development of energy conservation efforts there should be incentives and not disincentives established by the respective institution's central administration (Givens, 1995). During budget periods, it should be understood by senior level administrators that there might be additional costs incurred in the short term. However, savings realized by these projects, if allowed to remain under plant operations (versus allocated to other parts of the institutions), not only will cover the incremental cost, but will also serve to reduce overall operational expenses in the long run.

Other recommendations involve the development of a well-planned EMC program. Such a program, from (Karkia (1997) includes

- *Elements of success (management, productivity, energy and information systems),*
- *Strategic planning,*
- *Administrative steps,*
- *Technical steps.* (Karkia, 1997, pp. 1074–75).

For example, the Maricopa County Community College District in Arizona, the second-largest multicampus community college in the United States, developed an energy master plan in an effort to save $4.3 million on its utility bill (Zeloznicki, 2000). Its analysis included "a detailed evaluation covering existing equipment for efficiency, aging, and projected maintenance cost; user needs, desires, and goals; utility service providers, their rates and reliability; and load patterns based on current and projected consumption alternatives" (Zeloznicki, 2000, p. 39). San Diego State University in California saved in the range of $250,000 to $300,000 annually through an on-line control system that serves to automatically adjust building energy use (Sturgeon, 1998). Under strategic planning, the University of Texas in Houston found that assessment and evaluation of its utilities operations was critical to realizing substantial resource and financial savings (Yeoman, Palani, and McKee, 1998).

In a more comprehensive analysis from McIntyre (1995), the State University of New York at Stony Brook reveals how it began to plan strategically in the late 1980s for energy conservation in an effort to contain costs in plant operations that would eventually benefit the university system.

Stream Lining at Stony Brook

Officials at the State University of New York (SUNY) at Stony Brook had been thinking about constructing a cogeneration plant for the production of electricity and steam power since the early 1980s, according to Carl Hanes, deputy to the president for special projects. But the existing technology at the time made such a massive project unfeasible. Accordingly, there was limited access to natural gas on Long Island (where the Stony Brook campus is located). However, in 1987, the Iroquois Line, a major natural gas line, was constructed across the Long Island Sound. The line provided an adequate supply of natural gas to Long Island, and Stony Brook officials began to consider what future possibilities might be investigated. By 1988, it appeared that the technology had advanced and it had become financially feasible to take on this project. A feasibility study convinced Stony Brook officials that their campus was an ideal candidate for a cogeneration plant, in particular because of the substantial amount of steam the campus uses for both heating in the winter and cooling in the summer.

Using the study to convince state government officials and SUNY central administration officers that the project was feasible and financially attractive, Stony Brook officials eyed the $75 million projected cost (which eventually rose to $100 million) and tried to envision a financing package for their project. The SUNY system has a bond cap in effect for the entire system, and Stony Brook officials realized that the other campuses were unlikely to yield their portion of the bond limit for a major construction project at the Stony Brook campus. So Hanes and other Stony Brook officials sought to have the state energy laws changed. To permit financing by a long term-term construction contract by ensuring the state law was amended to allow a twenty-year contract, with three five-year renewal periods.

The contract also includes a provision that gives Stony Brook the right to authorize the use of excess energy by other SUNY institutions. While it is far too early to accurately estimate the financial benefits to the Stony Brook plant, there clearly are some non-fiscal advantages. SUNY now has triple redundancy for generating steam. Such a layering of back-ups is important in light of the hospital and nursing home Stony Brook operates. Environmental benefits are often intangible, but just as important. "The pollutants have been reduced by about 70 percent because the new process is much cleaner, and much more efficient." Moreover, the cogeneration plant *is just one element of an effort to improve energy efficiency at Stony Brook. "Our campus has been involved in many other energy efficient measures, and we anticipate that the energy savings will generate substantial savings in the future"* (McIntyre, 1995, pp. 30–31).

Both public and private institutions should be cognizant of their respective states' position on the deregulation of utility companies. California, New York and Pennsylvania are highlighted in Hunsicker (1998) as a result of their proactive roles in restructuring their respective utility industries over the last five-year period.

California State Initiatives on Utilities Deregulation

Pacific Gas and Electric Company, San Diego Gas and Electric Company, and Southern California Edison Company have been directed to restructure the electric utility industry in California. Such actions were initiated by the restructuring decision made by the California Public Utilities Commission and by restructuring legislation signed by Governor Pete Wilson on September 23, 1996. In broad terms, the implementation of the restructuring initiatives on the part of the aforementioned utilities companies have involved 1) delineating certain facilities as either local distribution facilities (subject to state jurisdiction) or transmission facilities subject to the FERC's jurisdiction, 2) conveying operational control of designated transmission faculties to an independent systems operator, and 3) applying to sell electric energy at market-based rates using power exchange. Under the utilities restructuring, the traditional market structure that features vertically integrated utilities (that is, utilities engaged in the generation, transmission, and distribution of electric power to customers in defined service territories at cost-of-service-based rates) will be replaced by a new market structure that allows for the sale of power by multiple sellers to retail distributors and end users at market rates. Such market based sales of power will be facilitated by nondiscriminatory transmission service providers under tariffs of general applicability administered by the independent system operator. To deal with utility stranded costs, a competitive transition charge will be calculated as a function of the difference between the generation component of the existing utility tariff and the power exchange price. To address regulatory concerns as to the utilities' market power in power generation markets, the utilities have agreed to divest themselves of significant portions of their fossil fuel generation capacity. The difference between the prices received for such plants and the utilities' book value of such plants will be subject to stranded cost recovery.

New York

As of early 1998, the New York Public Service Commission has approved restructuring plans submitted by Consolidated Edison, New York State Electric and Gas, Niagara Mohawk, Orange & Rockland, Rochester Gas and Electric, and Central Hudson. The method for recovery of stranded costs has not been finalized, however. Under the varying details of the utility-specific plans, retail competition will be available by a certain date, with different levels of guaranteed or expected rate decreases for . . . different customer classes. As indicated by filings submitted to the FERC, New York anticipates the establishment and implementation in 1998 of independent system operators that will be responsible for balancing load and electricity generation and the dispatch of electricity through a power exchange. Bills before the New York legislative call for full retail customer choice to be implemented by September 2000.

New York has experimented with pilot programs that could serve as useful models in other areas. One program, proposed by Dairylea Cooperative and approved by the New York Public Service Commission, includes dairy farmers and food processors in the service territories of the four largest utilities. Dairylea plans to purchase power for the aggregate needs of its members. Outside power suppliers or aggregators may compete against utilities for this power business. Dairylea has forecast that the pilot program will save end users 10 to 20 percent on their electricity rates. The New York State Public Service Commission also has approved certain arrangements whereby cogenerators have been permitted to sell retail power to nearby industrials. Depending on local laws, this example suggests that institutions in the other states may investigate whether cogeneration units can be installed to meet energy requirements, with excess power marketed to nearby industrial or commercial loads.

The feasibility of such approach seemingly will depend on state-specific issues such as the definition of public utility (i.e., Does an institution become a regulated public utility by selling power to end-users?) And the availability of the transmission and distribution services necessary to market power that is in excess of the institution's needs.

Pennsylvania

Pennsylvania passed legislation necessary to introduce retail electricity competition on December 3, 1996. The Electricity Generation Customer Service Choice and Competition Act will phase in retail competition beginning January 1, 1999. Rate caps ensure that utilities' captive and direct access customers will not experience rate increases. In addition, the Pennsylvania Public Utilities Commission is granted the authority to mandate pilot programs, approve utility restructuring plans, and make decisions concerning the recovery of stranded costs by the utilities.

In early 1998, the Pennsylvania Publics Utilities Commission approved a restructuring plan for PECO Energy Company that projects reductions in electric bills of up to 15 percent. The Public Utilities Commission was expected to issue orders on the restructuring plans submitted by all Pennsylvania utilities in summer 1998. Some indication of the potential vitality of retail electricity competition in Pennsylvania is afforded by reports that some 30 energy suppliers have been approved by the Public Utilities Commission to participate in Pennsylvania's pilot program for retail competition. However, recent events in Pennsylvania may have altered this direction (Hunsicker, 1998, pp. 45–48).

Currently, of the three states, California has experienced the worst reaction from its attempts at utility deregulation. In the short run, the wholesale price for electricity dramatically increased for the state's utility companies due in large part to three major areas: 1) above average increases in oil and natural gas prices; 2) a mandate from the state's deregulation plan for California utility companies to purchase power from the California Power Exchange, a consortium whose power rates are among the highest in the country; and 3) the absence of a newly developed utility infrastructure that could increase the state's power suppliers (O'Leary, 2000).

> *To understand what went wrong in California, it is necessary to review that state of the industry before the introduction of whole-sale competition in 1992. Partly because of the uncertainties created by the expectation that deregulation was coming, vertically integrated utilities were not building enough generation and transmission capacity during the 1990s to match the growth in demand. Industry observers offered many new different explanations for this lack of capacity, including local opposition to new plant construction, environmental concerns, incorrect demand forecast, a perceived glut of available power in some areas of the county, and regulatory refusal to offer satisfactory rates of return. In the end, it most likely was a combination of these and other factors that led traditional utilities to ratchet back on their power and plant construction budgets* (Fox-Penner and Basheda, 2001, p. 52).

Problems encountered by California have prompted many states to revisit their plans for utility deregulation. However, as with the initial deregulation of the phone and airline industries, the full impact of these policies on consumers was not felt for years. Consequently, this provides added incentive for college and university plant operations to develop energy management plans and to remain current on state legislative agendas concerning utility deregulation.

Summary

Plant operation expenditures represent approximately 6.6 percent and 6.1 percent of total expenditures in public and private four-year institutions, respectively. Over the past twenty years, colleges and universities neglected critical upkeep in plant operations and facilities in an effort to realize short-term cost savings. One method used to realize these short-term savings was to defer or delay scheduled maintenance work on buildings and equipment. It was estimated in 1995 that it would take roughly $26 billion to eliminate the accumulated deferred maintenance in colleges and universities. One of the recommendations in contending with deferred maintenance, from a cost containment perspective, included requiring a specific amount set aside for replacement of the physical plant at a specific replacement value percentage. In addition, outsourcing, which is the contracting out of university services to an outside vendor, has gained greater recognition as an efficient means of cost containment for certain plant operations and facilities management (for example, house and groundskeeping). Although outsourcing should not be used as a panacea for cost containment in plant operations, plant directors should first determine the actual cost differences between self-operation and contracting out the service before making a decision to outsource.

A last area for discussion of cost containment in plant operations has been the escalating expense in energy management. Each year, colleges and universities spend millions of dollars on electricity, natural gas, fuel oil, purchased steam, and other miscellaneous energy sources. Because electricity represents a central role in the energy cost structure, a great deal of attention has been given to the role deregulation of the electric utility industry will play in influencing these costs at colleges and universities. It has been argued that electricity prices are supposed to decrease as result of increased competition. If the state of California's experience with deregulation during spring 2001 becomes the norm, average utility costs for consumers will increase. However, the actual results from deregulation for both institutions and private industry will not be evident for some time due to the limited amount of knowledge, experience, and consistency regarding how the marketplace for energy will respond.

Is Research a Facilitator or Barrier to Cost Containment?

Sponsored Research

After World War II, the scholarship of discovery and the attendant focus on research became more widespread throughout America's institutions of higher education. It was then that universities began rewarding faculty for their ability to secure research funding and postsecondary institutions sought national recognition through their faculty's research accomplishments (Glassick and others,[1] 1997). In a fall 1992 essay, Joseph D. Duffey, who was then president of The American University, warned that cost containment efforts would come to define the operations and the goals of institutions of higher education. Duffey pointed to the 1980s as an anomalous time when American colleges and universities enjoyed their greatest prosperity, a prosperity that more currently has been severely diminished and which has resulted in a reexamination of university spending. As a result of the prosperity enjoyed in the 1980s, Duffey argued that

> [f]or the foreseeable future, the practical tasks for those engaged in higher education will first come down to cost containment efforts. In part, the adjustments we face are made more difficult by the experiences of the past decade. The 1980s were heady years for American higher education. As we attempted to shape up the curriculum with a return to the concept of general education, faculties at many universities turned over more teaching responsibilities to graduate students. The ranks of full-time faculty

increased significantly even as teaching loads were reduced. Staff and mid-level administrative positions proliferated. Many of our universities grew accustomed to annual budgets that were augmented by major overhead and indirect cost revenues from federally sponsored research. Throughout much of the decade, annual tuition increases at many private colleges and universities were twice the rate of inflation or greater (Duffey, 1992, p. 10).

And then as the economy lost momentum, these institutions faced the task of cutting back and reorganizing in order to avoid becoming overextended. Such efforts required, "in most instances, scaling back the expectations shaped by the steady increase in available resources through the 1980s" (Duffey, 1992, p. 10). Nowhere is the effort to scale back felt more fully than in the area of faculty research.

Each institution must evaluate the role research should play in its mission.

As a result of the ongoing efforts to contain costs, each institution must evaluate the role research should play in its mission. When evaluating the place of research in the academy, the following should be considered:

- Protection of incentives for researchers and research institutions;
- Support for research equipment and instrumentation;
- Support for research libraries;
- Allocation of funds for both basic and applied research;
- Attention to ethical and related concerns;
- The cost of losing out on other opportunities (Simpson, 1991).

The mission of a university determines many of the financial costs of that institution. There are many who argue that a number of institutions could, and should, save funds by redefining their mission and devoting their resources to teaching rather than to research. It is argued that "a significant number of the nation's 'regional' public doctoral-granting universities (as opposed to the nationally or internationally eminent public research universities) could teach students at a lower cost if they were to cease operating as research universities and if their faculty instead were given the high teaching loads characteristic of two- or four-year teaching colleges" (Johnstone, 1998, n.p.). However, such a change would not indubitably lead to a more productive institution. Such a change might result in

> *a fundamentally different kind of institution: cheaper in per-student costs perhaps (although low-cost graduate teaching assistants would no longer be available), but not necessarily cheaper in per-student learning. Unquestionably it would be less productive in scholarship and probably in service to the community. Again, this change would be not so much a radical shift in a pattern of finance as a radical redefinition of the very missions of these dozens or hundreds of institutions* (Johnstone, 1998, n.p.).

As such a discussion of altering the mission of the university in order to alter its costs and funding strategies makes clear, by and large, members of the academy and its external constituents have starkly different views of the role of the professorate and the mission of the academy. On the one hand, there have been repeated efforts on the part of the public to remind faculty members of their duty to one of their primary constituents—their students. To that end, the public has called for the professorate to pay greater attention to their teaching rather than to their research. On the other hand, faculty members regard their research as one of the primary contributions they make both to advancing the prestige of their individual institutions and to advancing the knowledge of the intellectual community at large. However, as Robert Rosenzweig points out, if one point of view were triumphant over another, such a triumph would result in producing

> *universities as different from today's as today's universities are from those of a century ago. More to the point, significant movement along that continuum in either direction would have profound consequences, as the postwar shift in the direction of research demonstrates. The conflict between teaching and research is one of several important points of tension that arise out of the conflict between what society wants from its universities and what it needs but may not recognize* (Rosenzweig, 1998, pp. 189).

The public perception of faculty teaching loads and productivity constitutes an ongoing issue. In particular, many members of the public are concerned about what appears to be a six- or eight-hour workweek. However, it has been found that most university faculty in research universities work very hard. The combination of faculty members' attention to teaching, preparation for teaching, graduate student supervision, research, university service, and professional obligations off campus have placed faculty in the same category as lawyers and doctors for the sheer number of hours worked (Rosenzweig, 1998). As a result, Rosenzweig observes that "[h]ard work is not the issue; how it is distributed is" (Rosenzweig, 1998, p. 164). Nonetheless, given that many believe that more and more of the responsibility for financing higher education—and in turn, financing research—has been placed on students and families rather than public and governmental sources, the public's misperception about faculty priorities are highly problematic.

University-Sponsored Research

In fact, a majority of faculty members regard published research as their primary responsibility to the academy. In a survey of 35,478 full-time faculty nationwide, UCLA's Higher Education Research Institute found that professors said their highest priority is to maintain the reputation of their respective institutions. In addition, economic development in many universities and colleges has been tied to successfully competing for research funding. However, the statutory, regulatory, and political environment is such that the government and society at large also are demanding greater accountability from postsecondary institutions—both in terms of how research funds are used and in terms of demonstrating the integrity of the institution's ongoing relationship with its students.

The financial well-being of colleges and universities, and research universities[2] in particular, are markedly sensitive to external factors. While it is clear that the policies of the national government are a matter of great concern, it also is worth noting that

> [f]*actors beyond the realm of academe, such as the costs of health care, building prisons, and balancing the national budget, are hav-*

ing a direct impact on outside revenue sources for colleges and universities. While certain of these pressures have been greater on some institutions than on others, virtually every institution with a sig-· nificant research component has witnessed a dramatic increase in competition for research dollars from all sources in recent years (Karr and Kelley, 1996, p. 37).

As a result of such competition, in recent years, the rejection rates for university and college research grant applications have increased dramatically (Karr and Kelley, 1996). Thus, strategic planning is vital in such a competitive environment and a scattershot approach to identifying and securing funding is neither efficient nor will such an approach make the institution appear particularly compelling in a highly selective competition (Karr and Kelley, 1996). Moreover, a scattershot approach could result in a precarious situation for ongoing research. Applications seeking funding to conduct research usually receive support without attention to continuing the support required for further basic research. Thus, care needs to be taken that funding for research is not turned on and off like a spigot without regard to the effect of holding a research team together or expanding the research over a larger continuum of time (Simpson, 1991).

Heightened competition also has prompted a shift in the types of research being conducted. This shift is characterized by a turn from basic curiosity-driven research to research that is more strategic or commercial in nature (see Sheila Slaughter and Larry L. Leslie (1997) *Academic Capitalism: Policies, Procedures, and the Entrepreneurial University*). Such a shift also counters the caveat that individual research should be evaluated in terms of the contributions it makes directly or indirectly to a faculty member's instructional performance. Finally, this shift has changed internal reward systems at some institutions of higher education. At some institutions, the entrepreneurialism evidenced by university units or individual faculty members is competitively encouraged and rewarded by remunerating those units and individuals who contain costs with supplementary funds. For example,

> [a]*t one institution, a percentage of each unit's central allocation was skimmed off the top at the beginning of the fiscal year, pooled*

together, and redistributed at the end of the year according to the unit's performance and the case it could make for being able to use the funds. Obviously, units that had performed well and planned to use funds for exciting projects or initiatives had a greater chance of receiving a larger portion of the pooled money (Karr and Kelley, 1996, p. 37).

The commercialization of faculty research has encouraged some administrators to regard faculty as academic entrepreneurs and knowledge as a form of venture capital (Blumenstyk, 2001). To that end, patents and royalties have become valuable revenue sources for institutions of higher education. For example, "Columbia ranked first among American universities in patent royalties for the past two years. Its royalty revenues for the 2000 fiscal year were more than $143 million. Columbia will almost certainly lead the pack again in 2001" (Blumenstyk, 2001, n.p.). Moreover, the money garnered from patent revenues often functions as an uncontrolled revenue stream. As Michael M. Crow, Columbia's executive vice provost, explains, the patent revenues generated by academic researchers at Columbia represent "the freest money we have" (Crow qtd. in Blumenstyk, 2001, n.p.) because the money comes without any of the oversight or restrictions that accompany research financed with government or corporate money.

In 1999, the debates concerning commercially sponsored academic research once again became heated as a result of a controversial agreement reached between the University of California, Berkeley and Novartis, a Swiss pharmaceutical company. The university granted Novartis "first right to negotiate licenses on roughly a third of the department's discoveries—including the results of research funded by state and federal sources as well as by Novartis" (Press and Washburn, 2000, n.p.). In addition, Berkeley offered the company "unprecedented representation—two of five seats—on the department's research committee, which determines how the money is spent" (Press and Washburn, 2000, n.p.). This arrangement called into question whether Berkeley was dedicated to conducting research dedicated to serving the public good. However, given that the rate of growth in federal support has continued to fall over the last twelve years, that state spending also has fallen, that the costs of conducting research have risen, and that the Bayh-Dole Act (enacted 1980, amended 1984) enabled universities to patent inventions made with government research money and to transfer those research results from universities to the commercial marketplace for the public benefit, like Berkeley, more and more universities are assuming those functions previously performed by industrial laboratories (Leslie and Slaughter, 1997; Press and Washburn, 2000).

Berkeley is not alone. Not only have a number of universities engaged in industry-sponsored research, but many also have allowed companies to endow chairs. For example, West Virginia University has a chair in the management school endowed by K-Mart while Freeport McMoRan, one of the world's largest copper and gold mining companies, has created a chair in environmental studies at Tulane (Press and Washburn, 2000). The corporate funding of academic research has raised questions about academic freedom, about the design of corporate-funded studies, and about what is published as a result of such studies (Cho and Bero, 1996). Moreover, "[a]ccording to the Association of University Technology Managers' annual report, dozens of major universities—Brandeis, West Virginia, Tufts, and Miami among them—actually spent more on legal fees in fiscal year 1997 than they earned from all licensing and patenting activity that year" (Press and Washburn, 2000, n.p.). Thus, as universities consider forging financial connections to industry, they need to evaluate not only the ethics of such alliances, but also the potential economic liabilities associated with protecting and defending their intellectual property vis a vis licenses, patents, and royalties.

Not only have a number of universities engaged in industry-sponsored research, but many also have allowed companies to endow chairs.

Direct and Indirect Cost Factors

In spite of the aforementioned concerns about the research missions of various institutions of higher learning or the types of research being funded, it is clear that research universities, and in particular, those with substantial research programs, receive annual payments totaling millions of dollars for the indirect costs associated with research sponsored by the government. In the recent past, such payments covered the cost of facilities, libraries, and utilities related to conducting the research. However, in 1996 the Clinton administration issued new rules that significantly changed the way the government reimburses universities for the overhead costs of federally supported research. In an effort to simplify reimbursement, the government dropped the term "indirect costs" from its overhead rules. The rules now divide overhead costs into two categories—research facilities and research administration. Now federal grants to universities also must conform to several major requirements of the Cost Accounting Standards Board, rules that previously applied to colleges only when they contracted with the government. As a result, research universities now argue, "the federal board's rules reduce the flexibility that institutions need in order to manage their costs wisely" (Cordes, 1996, p. A32).

There also are widespread concerns about earmarked appropriations. In order to ensure the quality of the research, it is widely believed that the competitive process of peer review should be consistently and conscientiously implemented. For example, some critics of earmarked appropriations "charge that earmarks are inequitable and can be a waste of taxpayer money because no experts review the projects to ensure that they match national spending priorities and are of high quality" (Brainard and Cordes, 1999, n.p.). Thus, rather than compromise merit to achieve geographic distribution on specialized projects via direct congressional appropriations, all research proposals should be ensured via peer review. And therefore, members of Congress and university presidents should refrain from awarding or seeking money for projects that evade the competitive merit-review process (Rosenzweig, 1998). To that end, whenever there is a need "to provide stimulus to particular localities, a separate program to support campus research facilities has been advocated by the Association of American Universities" (Cordes, 1988 qtd. in Simpson, 1991, p. 48). In spite of such recommendations, "[f]or the 2000 fiscal year, Congress directed federal agencies to award at least $1.044 billion for such projects—a 31-percent rise over last year's record total of $797 million" (Brainard and Southwick, 2000, n.p.).

Questions also have been raised as to whether mandatory cost sharing is appropriate or whether a greater recognition of the worth of the research function of universities should be encouraged. According to some, "[i]t is questionable whether it is appropriate to require universities to absorb part of the allowable total cost (direct and indirect) of federally sponsored research, considering that allowable cost is narrowly construed and fails to take into account much of the cost that a university incurs in order to be available as a not-for-profit research facility" (Simpson, 1991, p. 49). According to such an argument, because research universities are not-for-profit facilities whose findings "give rise to significant effects" (Simpson, 1991, p. 3) beyond the university proper, the local level, or the state level, they should be accorded greater latitude in terms of how they are funded.

A review of the literature identifies the following as the most pervasive pressures on institutions of higher learning: continuing resource constraints, demands for increased productivity and an attendant demonstration of that productivity, and an insistence on service to society and greater accountability. These pressures, by and large, are further complicated by: the demands of growing and diverse populations, faltering economies, rising costs in higher education, and a public that has become skeptical of the role and mission of institutions of higher learning. While it is clear that such pressures are pervasive, it also is clear that institutional decisions should not be made in response to the constraints themselves; rather, responses should be made proactively by establishing priorities through strategic planning. Following are some proactive strategies that have been implemented in strategic plans.

First and foremost, the faculty needs to be educated about budgets, and in particular, about how research funding is to be budgeted. For example, Robert Rosenzweig points out that "until recently, at least, in most universities educating the faculty about the economic condition of the university was not a high-priority item for administrations or for faculty" (Rosenzweig, 1998, p. 171). He goes on to explain that few faculty "had any real sense of where indirect cost recovery fit into the economics of the university—what the basis for recovery was, how it was calculated, where the money actually went, and why they did not see it directly in their own operations. For many, if not most, it was a mystery, and a somewhat sinister one at that" (Rosenzweig, 1998, p. 171).

Moreover, in the past, "research monies were plentiful, institutions placed the onus of grant-seeking squarely on individual faculty members. [However,] [t]he current funding climate makes this an unwise approach. Institutions that possess a strategic vision incorporating research activities are much more likely to cope effectively with a rapidly changing funding environment" (Karr and Kelley, 1996, p. 41). In addition, it should be noted that the chronic under-investment in physical plant maintenance (see "Can Plant Operations and Facilities Continue to Be Ignored?" on p. 49) may have constrained or compromised the capacity of many colleges and universities to conduct modern research. Not only is periodic maintenance required, but also existing facilities often need to be altered, or new ones built, to ensure that the necessary research equipment is available. Moreover, often "facilities must be updated to meet changing regulatory codes (such as animal care facilities)" (Gobstein, 1986, p. 251) as well as health and safety codes.

In *Tuition Rising: Why Colleges Costs So Much* (2000), Ronald Ehrenberg explains that one of the reasons faculty remain unclear about the economic conditions of their colleges and universities as a whole is due, in part, to the fact that individual colleges or academic units are budgeted independently and competitively. Ehrenberg argues that maintaining central control over all budgetary resources coupled with rewarding cooperation between university units for resources would aid institutions of higher learning to become more economically efficient and make the hard choices in order to contain costs. One means of coping effectively with a changing funding environment is to encourage more interdisciplinary research. "Universities can help promote interdisciplinary research through a number of avenues, the most obvious of which is financial support" (Karr and Kelley, 1996, p. 37). Other promotional techniques also can be implemented. For example, "[a] prestigious southern research university, recognizing that interdisciplinary activities needed space in order to thrive, created a building designed specifically to bring together members from widely different departments" (Karr and Kelley, 1996, p. 37). Not only do such efforts help to overcome fragmentation and balkanization among academic communities, but they also encourage innovative and thus competitive forms of research.

Furthermore, faculty members should recognize when there is a logical connection between weaker and stronger academic units and when it would be highly cost effective to merge the units (Karr and Kelley, 1996). For example, merging a weak math department with a strong physics department could yield a stronger academic unit and could result in more competitive research opportunities. Moreover, it has been found that decreasing the size of graduate programs also can be seen as a positive move, "especially when graduates with doctoral degrees are unemployed or underemployed. Additionally, paring down overly large programs may help strengthen them by freeing up funds to support students at more attractive levels" (Karr and Kelley, 1996, p. 38).

However, when paring down a graduate program, the faculty must ensure continued quality research. To that end, interdisciplinary research may prove helpful, as it would be possible to pool graduate students as well as other resources. In addition, "researchers may find some relief in using undergraduates for certain research activities" (Karr and Kelley, 1996, p. 39). Also, integrating undergraduates into research activities would help to nullify the perception that faculty members are not spending adequate time with the undergraduate members of the student population. The use of undergraduates would provide for closer working relationships between faculty members and undergraduates—a provision that would help to improve the public perception of the faculty's investment in undergraduate education.

Integrating undergraduates into research activities would help to nullify the perception that faculty members are not spending adequate time with the undergraduate members of the student population.

In addition, business partnerships should be investigated and encouraged as the university and the business could share the costs of the project and the potential revenues. While corporate-university research partnerships will become an increasingly important means to secure research monies, such partnerships will need to be developed judiciously. An oft-cited story of how such partnerships may not prove to be mutually beneficial is well worth repeating here. On April 25, 1996, a *Wall Street Journal* story reported that an article that had been accepted for publication by the *Journal of the American Medical Association* on a research study conducted at the University of California at San Francisco had been withdrawn because a drug company prohibited the writers from publishing their results. Believing its more expensive drug would be found superior to others, the drug company had paid for a university study of its drug as it compared to its competitor's cheaper versions. However, when the study found that the company's drug was indistinguishable from those of the competition, the company prohibited publication of any results of the study, citing a clause in its contract with the university giving it the right to do so. The university complied with the contract (King, 1996).

According to Dr. Marcia Angell, such cases are becoming all too common. Dr. Angell, former editor of *The New England Journal of Medicine,* warns that if researchers and their universities develop financial connections to industry, they may discover that such connections will interfere with the kinds of independent inquiry that are expected from academic research. Moreover, she argues, "the search for truth is giving way to the search for profits" (qtd. in Blumenstyk, 2000, n.p.). For, as she contends, to maintain corporate sponsorship, academic researchers may suppress negative studies, or worse yet, convert negative studies into positives (see Blumenstyk, 2000, n.p.). Thus, if researchers want to maintain a capital base necessary to perform quality research, they must be creative in their applications for funding, strategic in their conceptualization of research projects, and ethical in minimizing any conflicts of interest in seeking sponsorship for their research projects.

Summary

External support for university research began as "small endowments and government appropriations for agricultural experiment stations" (The National Academy of the Sciences, 1989); however, the autonomy of the academy has been threatened as colleges and universities become more and more dependent on external funding—findings that have grown into a multibillion-dollar enterprise (Yudof, 1992). When universities accept money from external sources, they may compromise their ability to conduct research that generates new discoveries and new knowledge and that promotes the public good. Instead, universities may feel more and more compelled to conduct research with industrial relevance in order to win state, federal, foundation, and private funding.

The efforts to contain costs significantly influence the extent to which faculty are able to conduct academic research. Because providing incentives for research activity, supporting research facilities (including equipment, instrumentation, libraries, and the collection and dissemination of information), and allocating funds for both applied and basic research are costly, each institution of higher learning must evaluate the role research can play and should play in its mission. Those institutions that regard research as central to their mission must negotiate the public perception that research comes at the cost of teaching. These institutions would be well advised to fully justify all research costs and, whenever possible, to integrate undergraduate students into research activities. Institutions dedicated to research need to recognize how to address increased competition for both internal funding as well as external state, federal, or private funding. Institutions dedicated to research also must investigate how to manage their costs wisely to meet the requirements imposed by federal grants—especially when mandatory cost sharing regulates those expenses. Successful research institutions should ensure that strategic planning is instituted to make certain that academic research does not detract from the academy's educational goals. To that end, whenever possible, researchers should be encouraged to conduct interdisciplinary research, to integrate both undergraduate and graduate students into the research project, and to be judicious in their use of external sponsors or partners (and in particular to be cautious in their use of corporate sponsors). Finally, academic units should be encouraged to function less independently of one another because a shared mission and shared governance makes the reallocation of resources and streaming of programs not only possible but productive.

Can University Student Services
Remain Viable with an Increasing
Cost Structure?

INCREASINGLY, INSTITUTIONS OF HIGHER EDUCATION are losing out to other institutions supported by state and federal funds—institutions that make competing demands on public resources (such as corrections facilities). As a result of such competition, higher-education institutions need to establish themselves as a primary state and federal priority to ensure they receive their share of necessary resources. To that end, colleges and universities must strengthen the public's image of higher education by enabling the public to more fully understand the causes for increased expenditures in the higher-education sector (Leslie and Rhoades, 1995). According to Leslie and Rhoades, colleges and universities need to address the allegations that undergraduate education is not being attended to adequately, that tuition prices continue to rise and it isn't apparent that higher prices have translated into

> **Higher-education institutions need to establish themselves as a primary state and federal priority to ensure they receive their share of necessary resources.**

higher educational opportunities for students, and that higher education has become inefficient in its use of public resources (Leslie and Rhoades, 1995). In particular institutions of higher learning need to explain increases in administrative expenditures, especially because administrative costs have outpaced instructional costs (Leslie and Rhoades, 1995). Given that the public maintains a relatively uncomplicated view of the complex operations of institutions of higher learning, a good deal more needs to be done to effectively address recurrent criticisms—such as criticisms directed at administrative costs—by ensuring that cost increases are explained using hard data and that escalations in costs are fully justified.

At private institutions, tuition once claimed 20 to 25 percent of an average family income; today tuition claims up to 50 percent and beyond. And at state institutions, when state governments refuse to increase funding resources, many believe that the higher-education institutions in those states pass on the deficit to students in the form of setting higher fees. In fact, according to some, "fees are generally treated by colleges as a stable source of revenue when the state doesn't come through" (Carnevale, 1999, n.p.). Moreover, many believe that "[t]he ability of students and families to cover increasing costs of higher education out of savings, current income, or increased debt has all but evaporated, and the burden of debt is diminishing the capacity of governments, families, and students to cover the cost of higher education" (Garland and Grace, 1993, pp. 13–14).

It is within such a climate that colleges and universities must justify their current costs and attempt to contain those costs while also increasing their market share. To increase their market share, institutions need to determine prospective students' desires and then to deliver on students' requests. To that end, many institutions compete on offering everything from advanced amenities of student life[3] to relaxing requirements for admission (Simpson, 1991) to offering financial assistance in the form of both need-based and merit-based aid. In addition to attracting students, colleges and universities must ensure that they keep those whom they do attract, as there have been growing concerns about the escalation in attrition rates in higher education. The aforementioned concerns are those that must be addressed by the administrators and staff members who work in student services.

To deliver the services requisite to secure the desired level of student enrollments, institutions must engage in long-range strategic planning to determine where the institution is now and where it wants to be in the future. "The framework components of long-range planning—mission statement, objectives, programs, organization, personnel resources, facilities resources, and financial resources—must be constantly evaluated and updated as indicated by feedback" (Boer, 1979, n.p.). Moreover, according to Boer, "[t]he student personnel function is key to the survival of a college or university since the recruitment, admission, and retention of students will determine to a large extent the future of the institution" (Boer, 1979, n.p.). However, while it may be that the growth in student services came about when the competition for students grew more intense, it also is true that student services has been one of the places hardest hit during budget cuts. First, for the most part, similar to the majority of administrators, the administrators who staff student services do not have tenure; thus in times of retrenchment, the positions of student services personnel are not secure. Second, no matter how important their services may be, these personnel are not the reason for the institution's existence. Nonetheless, to remain competitive, as Boer argues, student services personnel are key to the survival of the institution, and to that end it is vital that institutions evaluate how best to provide skilled and competitive student services while also remaining cost efficient. It also is vital to recognize that student affairs professionals make an invaluable contribution in creating and maintaining an effective living and learning environment for students that ensures their retention, and thus ensures greater cost effectiveness on the part of the university as a whole.

Student Aid Administration

All student affairs professionals are under pressure to demonstrate their accountability to legislators, parents, alumni, and regulatory bodies. On the front lines are the professionals in the Office of Admissions and the Office of the Registrar.[4] The Office of Admissions is held accountable for preparing publications for admissions packages and then for evaluating the cycle of time from inquiry to response-to-request. The Office of the Registrar is responsible for registering credits, evaluating credits for transfer students, recording grades, processing transcript requests, and issuing grade reports. To concurrently improve the quality and reduce the costs, many colleges and universities have automated a number of the services provided. Such automation requires the training of key personnel and vigilance in preparing for the integration of emerging technologies.

An example of such automation is underway at the University System of Georgia where online student services allows students to go one place to apply to the system's thirty-four public colleges and universities, find information and guidance on financial aid, register for courses, find library resources (many of which are in digital format), and get help with career placement through a job hunting database (Carnevale, 2000). The one-stop, online approach to student services is now becoming routine. However, while such online services have become part of the daily operations of the university, their attendant costs remain worrisome.

> **The one-stop, online approach to student services is now becoming routine. However, the attendant costs remain worrisome.**

In addition to enhancing their use of costly electronic services, institutions also are called upon to expend increasing amounts of money and time in attending to state and federal regulations and statutes, and it is student services personnel who often are held responsible for monitoring institutional compliance. In recent years there have been significant legislative actions and laws that affect campus operations. In particular, affirmative action, the civil rights codes, the First Amendment, the Americans with Disabilities Act, financial aid, and sexual harassment regulations prohibit discrimination against certain groups of people or require affirmative actions on the part of institutions of higher education. Of greatest significance to the majority of institutions is the requirement that those institutions of higher education that receive federal financial aid assistance "follow not only the programmatic and technical requirements of each program under which aid is received but also various civil rights requirements that apply generally to federal aid programs" (Kaplin and Lee, 1997, p. 544). In particular, colleges and universities are bound by Title VI of the Civil Rights Act of 1964 that states that "[n]o person in the United States shall, on the ground of race, color, or national origin, be excluded from participation in, be denied the benefits of, or be subjected to discrimination under any program or activity receiving federal financial assistance." Title IX of the Education Amendments of 1972 states that "no person in the United States shall, on the bias of sex, be excluded from participation, be denied the benefits of, or be subject to discrimination under any educational programs or activity receiving federal financial assistance"; Section 504 of the Rehabilitation Act of 1973 prohibiting disability discrimination, The Age Discrimination Act of 1975, and Title II of the Americans with Disabilities Act prohibit discrimination by public entities.

One of the key services provided by student services personnel is the administration of student aid. At the campus level, financial aid incurs a redistribution of tuition dollars that must be carefully accounted for. The most obvious source of income for any institution is the tuition it charges its students to attend. Virtually all institutions—both public and private—raised their tuition rates during the 1980s when there was a growth in income and again during the 1990s in response to cost constraints produced, in part, by inflation. However, tuition cannot repeatedly be called upon to bear the burden of increased institutional expenses. The cause-and-effect relationship between increases in financial aid and the attendant increases in tuition are understood differently by different theorists.

1. Some believe that private and public institutions have responded to the external sources, and in particular the decline in external funding—such as federal funding—by increasing the amount of money they spend on financial aid that in turn stimulates tuition increases.
2. Some believe that it is a problem with internal finances that causes the problem; that is, they believe that while tuition increases may address the problem of increased and increasing operating costs, they also lead to an increased demand for institutional financial aid.
3. Others theorize that higher tuition and a greater demand for financial aid are part of a cycle of rising costs. According to this theory, "costs will rise to equal all tuition, endowment, state appropriations, federal government grants, and other income sources available" (Morgan, 1983, p. 283). That is to say, tuition levels rise in order to capture the available federal funds, scholarship funds, and loans.

Many believe that the high tuition/high aid strategy is meant to benefit needy students. However, in his review of the policies of fifty states, Lenth found that only twenty-five states had explicit policies whereby tuition increases would be offset by increases in grant awards to needy students. And of the twenty-five, only one of the state grant programs—New York's—provided for need-based entitlements. In addition, he found that the same fiscal pressures that cause states to cut back on funding for state institutions also affect spending on financial aid (Lenth, 1993).

Moreover, the belief that financial aid will provide greater access to minority students also needs to be more fully scrutinized. Recent studies indicate that financial aid that does target minority students may not be achieving all that it should. Rather than providing access for a greater number of students, it may only be providing more institutional choice for a few. As Howard-Hamilton and others argue,

> [m]*uch emphasis has been placed on the use of minority scholarships to increase the number of minority students attending institutions of higher education. Because minority scholarships are merit-based, they often serve as a tool to attract qualified minority applicants to one school over another rather than to increase the number of minority students actually participating in higher education* (Howard-Hamilton and others, 1998, p. 53).

Furthermore, as these researchers point out, because it has been found that academic ability—rather than socioeconomic status—is the strongest predictor as to whether one will attend college "[t]he potential influence of financial assistance on college attendance is not as critical for high-ability students as it is for middle-ability students" (Howard-Hamilton and others, 1998, p. 53). Therefore, the financial aid that it is awarded may not be reaching the pool of candidates for whom it was intended.

The discussion of financial aid is compounded by the fact that in the 1980s there was a pronounced shift from awarding grants to furnishing loans. This shift also contributed to the decrease in minority enrollments and to the increase in defaults on student loans—especially for students of low-income families (Waggaman, 1991).

It is also worth noting that as long as there is demand for places at the country's elite institutions, costs will continue to rise and the competition for the top students will continue to influence the way colleges think about the role of student aid (in particular, the rise of merit-based rather than need-based aid) (Clotfelter, 1996; Ehrenberg, 2000; Frank, 1999; Hoxby, 2000; Huber,

1992; McPherson and Schapiro, 1998). Ronald Ehrenberg (2000) argues that the economic return in attending a selective institution is so pronounced that elite institutions are not compelled to make more decisions or to develop economically efficient practices; as a result, tuition will continue to rise. Ehrenberg also expresses his concern that as the competition for the top students continues, the rise of merit-aid will erode elite institutions' commitment to need-based financial aid. Robert Frank explains, "The fact that elite schools are increasingly the gateway to professional positions offering six-figure starting salaries has fueled the explosive growth in demand for elite educational credentials" (p. 9). And to be in demand, one must garner high rankings. For example, Frank notes, "when Cornell's Johnson Graduate School of Management jumped from eighteenth to eighth in the *Business Week* rankings in 1998 (the largest advance in the poll's history), applicants for the following year's class rose more than 50 percent" (p. 9).

While the pool of applicants might have grown dramatically, it is important to recognize that elite institutions want to attract the best and brightest students in the nation. To do so, selective institutions pay high salaries to attract and to keep distinguished, highly visible faculty who will attract students. The institutions also spend a great deal of money to convince students to attend their school—from expensive mailings to get them enrolled in the college to extensive upgrades of the campus amenities to keep them at the institutions. Moreover, as Michael McPherson and Morton Owen Schapiro warn, this competition to attract the best students has influenced how elite colleges and universities think about the role of financial aid because more and more of the elites have devoted financial resources to merit (rather than need-based) aid as a means of trying to attract top students whose families would not qualify for need-based money. As a consequence, McPherson and Schapiro contend that the federal government needs to be vigilant about ensuring access to college for needy students. They also call upon elite universities to restrain their urge for strategic advantage—an urge Frank (1999) refers to as a winner-take-all market for specific ivy-league schools. Frank further counsels elites to create collusive agreements that would compel these selective institutions to be more constrained in their expenditures, and more specifically, to limit their financial investment in attracting the best students.

To that end, the select colleges and universities need to interrogate a growing trend in regarding merit-based aid as an institutional responsibility.

These concerns about costs escalation should be tempered by the fact that private four-year colleges "enroll only 25 percent of all four-year college students" (Kane, 1997, p. 337), and elite colleges and universities represent an even smaller portion of that 25 percent. In addition, the recent developments at Princeton University indicate that necessary changes already are underway. According to a recent *Chronicle of Higher Education* report,

> *Beginning this fall [2001], Princeton undergraduates who receive financial aid will no longer be required to take loans out to help pay for their education and will instead receive larger grants from the university. Under the new policy, incoming students could graduate debt-free, instead of owing $15,000 to $20,000 or more at the end of four years. Officials expect the policy change, which they say may be the first of its kind, will affect nearly 25 percent of Princeton's undergraduates* (Olsen, 2001, n.p.).

The money to replace loans comes from the university's endowment income, and the trustees' choice to use the money in this way marks a promising beginning in what may become more widespread efforts to revisit cost structures and the use of financial aid at the nation's elite universities and colleges.

As this overview indicates, there needs to be a change in the basis on which financial aid is extended and a change in targeting to whom it will be awarded.

There needs to be a change in the basis on which financial aid is extended and a change in targeting to whom it will be awarded.

Some argue that the use of loans should be preferred to grants because "the use of loans recycles financial aid funds and conserves a college or university's resources, as well as the resources of the state and federal government" (Simpson, 1991, p. 73). Given that the right type of aid facilitates students' persistence in higher education, institutions of higher learning need to evaluate how best to provide greater access to their institution; how best to encourage a diverse community of students (including minority students, under-represented students, and rural students) to enroll; and how best to retain those students who require financial assistance.

Some institutions have been highly resourceful in reducing institutional costs as well as the cost to institutions of providing financial aid. Institutions such as Alice Lloyd, Berea, Blackburn, Warren Wilson, and the School of the Ozarks require students to perform unpaid services to the institution. As a condition for admission, each student is required to contribute a specified number of hours of unpaid on-campus service. For example, at Alice Lloyd College, "[w]ork is required of all full-time students to help with educational costs. Most students must work 10 hours a week on campus, engaged in such jobs as filing in the registrar's office, washing dishes in the kitchen, tutoring, and maintenance or grounds work. They are paid minimum wages which are applied to educational expenses" (Stepp, n.p.). Similarly, Warren Wilson requires that "[e]very student must work 15 hours a week, regardless of his or her financial need. In return, the Work Program compensates [the student] over $2000, which is deducted from the total cost of attending Warren Wilson" (Warren Wilson College, n.p.).

Student Activities

Student services also provide a number of ongoing services that are indispensable to the retention of students. However, those costs that are not associated with instructional costs often are considered expendable services. There is a growing "concern over the increasing allocation of higher education's resources away from instruction to institutional administration" (Leslie and Rhoades, 1995, p. 188). Leslie and Rhoades assume that "administrative costs generally are taken to be either institutional support or the combination of institutional support, academic support (minus libraries), and student services" (Leslie and Rhoades, 1995, p. 189).

Nevertheless, in order to retain students, quality student services must be implemented. For example, it has been found that orientation programs reduce student attrition. When it comes to preventing attrition, it has been found that orientation programs can be a first line of defense because they provide students with information that will aid them in adjusting to a new academic and social life. To that end, successful programs offer incoming students the following: information about financial aid; full descriptions of individual courses and academic programs; information about how to become a member of campus organizations; opportunities to establish working relationships with faculty members; services to aid students in establishing their interests and realizing their abilities; and assistance with their initial adjustment to and ongoing efforts to succeed in their academic life (Coll and Von Seggern, 1991). It has been found that students who participate in orientation programs are more likely to pass their first-term courses. Students who participate in orientation programs have improved performance regardless of a wide variety of factors predictive of attrition, such as age, gender, race, major, entrance examination scores, or employment status. Such improved performance is highly encouraging in terms of long-term retention of all students and of at-risk students in particular (Brawer, 1996). In addition, studies have shown that when faculty mentoring is combined with orientation programs, the return rate of students is even more pronounced. A system of academic advising that is widely recommended is one of shared advising relationships wherein students are provided opportunities and encouraged to work with a wide variety of individuals at the college in order to become acquainted with various members of the college community and to seek out the best advice in response to their proposed academic program (Frost, 1991).

As the example of orientation programs indicates, student services are not only important for securing one's market share and for developing a diverse community of students, student services are the very means of ensuring that the institution will retain those students it has attracted. While there are some predictive characteristics of those who have a higher dropout rate—for example, full- or part-time attendance, age, employment status, grade point average, financial concerns, being a member of an ethnic minority other than Asian, family obligations, and gender—rather than trying to predict dropout rates it is more productive to engage in intervention strategies to encourage retention. To that end, providing services such as orienta-

Student services are the very means of ensuring that the institution will retain those students it has attracted.

tion programs, faculty and peer mentoring, freshman seminars, women's centers, college-funded work-study programs, and academic-support programs are vital to students.

Supplemental Educational Services

One of the growing concerns for student-services professionals is the declining level of academic preparedness on the part of incoming students. This lack of preparedness not only has led to greater emphasis on remedial work, but also, arguably, to an easing of expectations and standards for entering students. Many argue that students' preparedness for entrance into college needs to be more fully assessed to ensure that remediation occurs before college. They argue "a distinction should be made between deficiencies in basic competencies in language and mathematics and deficiencies in study skills and in adapting to the college academic environment" (Simpson, 1991, p. 64). They believe basic competencies must be adhered to in admitting students to institutions of higher learning to ensure that remedial costs are kept down. Accordingly, basic competencies must be enforced to ensure that remedial costs are kept down and that underpreparation of students is addressed at the high-school level.

One means of assessing preparedness while potential students still are in high school is to ensure that, as an ongoing project, universities willingly work with the lower schools to improve elementary and secondary school education that will, in turn, lessen the requirements for remediation. Another solution is to encourage underprepared students to attend community colleges first. This solution necessitates encouraging community colleges to adopt remediation as one of their primary missions and necessitates stronger affiliations with community colleges in order to encourage their students to transfer to four-year institutions.

Nonetheless, once admitted to a four-year institution, students should be afforded a supportive learning environment. At present, academically underprepared students constitute one of the largest and fastest growing student populations on college campuses nationwide. Past studies have repeatedly indicated that nontraditional students needed additional academic support; however, more recent studies indicate that an increasing number of traditional students also are in need of remedial programs (Astin, 1993). Until higher levels of preparedness are reached, the costs of remediation need to be addressed on the college level as well. Moreover,

> [i]*n addition to remedial programs designed to address basic study skills in math and writing, poorly prepared students need educational and career counseling that seeks to match ability and aspirations. Developing efforts to address an increasing number of students who need help in developing skills is becoming increasingly important in institutions' efforts to retain students.* (Garland and Grace, 1993, pp. 35–36).

One means of providing the many services required is to consider consortia initiatives, because a sharing of resources benefits individual institutions while reducing costs. For example, Emmanuel College, Simmons College, Wheelock College, the Massachusetts College of Pharmacy and Allied Health Services, and the Wentworth Institute of Technology affiliated in order to achieve a collective benefit from sharing resources. In affiliating, the "Fenway five"—all of which are within a ten-minute walk of one another—will achieve savings through judicious joint-purchasing arrangements, more efficiently offering courses, purchasing student health insurance together, and combining campus security and food services expenses (Nicklin, 1996). As the president of Emmanuel College explained, the Fenway five, like other small colleges, were having "a tougher time recruiting students and fulfilling their academic goals and financial needs while making ends meet" (Nicklin, 1996, p. A34). As a result of their affiliation, they now are in a position to address shifts in student enrollments and students' demands or needs. Each college continues to maintain its own budget, its own faculty and administrators, and continues to set its own tuition. One of the more intriguing points about this affiliation between the five colleges is that officials of the colleges say their plan wouldn't hold as much promise if the institutions weren't so different. Emmanuel is a Catholic women's liberal-arts college that currently is going co-ed; the Massachusetts College of Pharmacy offers degrees in chemistry and nursing; Simmons is a women's liberal-arts college that offers doctoral degrees;

Wheelock is noted for its program in early-childhood education; and Wentworth focuses on engineering and mathematics (Nicklin, 1996).

In addition to investigating creative collaborative cost-saving efforts, privatization or outsourcing of services is one option embraced on many college campuses as the use of outside vendors allows for savings in personnel costs, service delivery, and equipment. (See "Can Plant Operations and Facilities Continue to Be Ignored?" on p. 49 for a more extensive discussion of the costs and benefits of outsourcing.)

As the aforementioned examples make clear, if institutions of higher learning want to maintain their market share and want to meet their mission, rather than cutting student services during times of financial tribulation, colleges and universities must seek creative solutions that allow for quality services while ensuring that costs are contained.

Summary

As the labor market for a college education has increased, college enrollment rates have risen. However, in the past two decades college tuitions have risen sharply as well. Such increases in institutional costs have led to increases in students' demands for institutional financial aid. Moreover, there is a widespread interest in clarifying how colleges and universities justify their escalating costs and also demonstrate a verifiable ability to provide access for students of all backgrounds to enjoy a college education. To that end, those who provide admission services must be knowledgeable about complicated loan systems and must be creative in the ways they create financial aid packages. Thus, one of the primary functions of the student services sector is to assist not only in attracting students to the college, but also to ensure that they are able to pay for their education once they have accepted. The student services sector provides a wide array of assistance to students, and many of its programs are threatened when there are constraints in what can be funded. Given that its programs may be the first to be cut back or cut altogether, those involved in student services continually must demonstrate the importance of the various programs they offer—from orientation programs to remediation for both traditional and nontraditional students. They also must seek ways to cut costs;

to that end, whenever it would not compromise the quality of the services being provided, the potential success of implementing automation, outsourcing, forming partnerships, and instituting consortia initiatives should be evaluated and implemented when deemed fitting.

External Cost Factors: Are States' Policies for Higher Education Institutions Helping or Hindering Cost Containment Opportunities?

FOUR-YEAR PUBLIC INSTITUTIONS traditionally have been exposed to external factors and influences outside the sphere of their control; these external factors and influences have had some impact on each institution's ability to secure additional revenues and consequently to manage costs. As a result, the financial health of these institutions is contingent upon the economic well-being of the state where they reside in addition to the respective public policy for higher education (Nettles and Cole, 2001). Within this context, state colleges and universities view the quality of their education in relationship to staffing ratios, funding and salary levels, selectivity in admissions, support of research and graduate programs, and the processes of shared governance (Richardson, Bracco, Callan, and Finney, 1998). In contrast, the general public's view of the quality of their state institutions resides more with performance and outputs indicators as evidenced by graduation rates and job opportunities. Consequently, it has been left up to state policy makers to attempt to balance the oftentimes-competing interests of institutional mission, market forces, and public interest. The states' ability to respond to these factors has either a direct or indirect impact on cost containment efforts at their respective public institutions.

It was predicted almost twenty years ago that higher education would cost more, that there would be stiff competition for state resources, that productivity would be difficult to increase, and that the socioeconomic benefits would be questioned (Glenny and Schmidtlein, 1980). Even though, over the last five to seven years, most states have been experiencing solid economic growth as result of a robust economy, institutions have had to compete for their share of revenue with other sectors. The heightened awareness of the funding needs of elementary and secondary education as a result of school reform, in addition to other mandated state functions such as health care and corrections, has reduced higher education's share of the revenue pie (Zumeta and Fawcett-Long, 1996). As a result,

- State appropriations for higher education increased by 7.1 percent from 1998-99 to 1999-2000, to a record $56.7 billion. Nearly every state posted spending increases above the rate of inflation during this period, and nine states reported double-digit increases in their appropriations. Over the past five years, the average annual increase in state spending in higher education has been 5.8 percent.
- While overall state funding of colleges and universities rose substantially since the 1990-92 recession, higher education's share of state funding has failed to recover its pre-recession levels. The portion of state general funds allocated to higher education stood at 13 percent in the 1999 fiscal year, compared with 15.2 percent in the 1989 fiscal year. Over the same period, the portion of state general funds allocated to Medicaid increased from 9 percent to 14 percent.
- While states' citizens have become wealthier, the portion of personal income allocated to higher education has declined. From academic year 1990-91 to 1999-2000, overall state higher-education appropriations per $1,000 of personal income fell from $9.39 to $8. During this period, only two states—Arkansas and Mississippi—posted increases in this area (American Association of State Colleges and Universities, 2000).

In the twenty-first century, states are expecting a surge in undergraduate enrollment from high school graduates who will represent a diverse segment of the population. Significant increases in students eligible for college enrollment are projected to come primarily from the eastern and western parts of the United States. For example, Nevada is expecting an 80 percent increase in high school graduates, California and Florida a 50 percent increase, with other states averaging increases between 10 to 20 percent (Western Interstate

Commission, 1998). This increase in eligible students will place additional pressure on resources that already are stretched to capacity in attempting to accommodate current enrollments. Therefore, more purposefully connecting the funding relationship between state governments and colleges and universities while also accounting for the fundamental effect on their cost structure is critical.

The expected relationship between state policy makers and public institutions has been viewed as a joint venture in the decision-making process for determining need (Hines, 1988). Within this decision-making process, state policy makers may include specific groupings of environmental factors, historical, political, economic, and demographic considerations (Lyddon, Fonte, and Miller, 1986). These components could be used to determine recommended funding allocations and assist in the evaluation of outcomes. Some of the other considerations include the call for performance-based funding and budgeting, meeting the accountability and assessment pressures requested by legislators and state governing boards, and the effect of restructuring to assure correct mission fulfillment. Consequently, the authors argue that state policy makers may not always be cognizant of whether their policy actions contribute to cost containment at the institutional level or act as barriers that create less opportunity for these institutions to operate more efficiently.

The situation becomes even more difficult to assess when the relationship between states and institutions varies depending on the type of span of control (governance structures) states exert over their colleges and universities (Layzell, 1996). For example, by the early 1970s, categorizations of governance structures in fifty states included

- States that have no coordinating structure.
- States that formed voluntary associations with varying degrees of coordinating activities.
- States with mandated advisory coordinating agencies that provide advice on policy issues but do not supplant the institution or system board authority.

- States that have regulatory coordinating agencies with absolute approval on selective policy issues.
- States with consolidated governing boards (Berdahl, 1974).

Assessment and Accountability

Assessment and accountability in state four-year institutions has been of paramount importance to lawmakers, state executives, and to the general public (Stevens and Hamlett, 1983). Regional accrediting associations also are placing demands on state institutions to produce evidence of positive outcome assessment (Derlin, 1996). Assessment, by and large, relies upon evaluations of student and program performance rather than on the current reputation of the institution (Bogue, 1998). Accountability, on the other hand, deals with the allocation of resources to those programs that experience positive outcomes in relationship to specific goals set by the institution or set by external bodies (Zumeta, 2000). The issue of accountability became paramount in the 1980s when questions were repeatedly posed to state institutions concerning educational quality, undergraduate instruction, and assessment of teaching and learning (Neal, 1995). Concern was fueled in large part by one publication: "A Nation at Risk (1983)." The study characterized America's youth as ill prepared, especially in terms of the results indicated by standardized international assessments and national college and university exams—assessments and exams which indicate a less than stellar performance on the part of American youth. The study of student performance on college and university exams addressed problematic conditions in two- and four-year state institutions. Findings also suggested that high schools needed to provide better preparation for college bound students and that institutions needed to provide greater student access to higher education. Emphasis had to be placed on what colleges and universities were doing in response to what graduates have learned and skills level achievement (Wingspread Report, 1993). In order to better evaluate the

High schools need to provide better preparation for college bound students and institutions need to provide greater student access to higher education.

achievement levels of their students, the majority of the states created assessment policies for their respective institutions during the 1980s (Dill, 1995). This response was characterized as a "campus-based approach," because colleges and universities had taken the lead in developing their own models for assessing institutional effectiveness as opposed to adhering to external models (Nettles, 1995; Ruppert, 1995). Nevertheless, this approach left many unanswered questions regarding whether there was actual evidence of improvements and whether more specific issues concerning college affordability, budget shortfalls, and equity were being addressed (Ruppert, 1995). More recently, accountability policies have shifted to accommodate more inclusiveness in the formation of assessment variables while also accounting for external constituency needs.

> *The new accountability policies of the mid-90s also bear less resemblance to the largely campus-based self-assessment approaches conceived as part of state level accountability policies of a decade ago. Rather, recent legislative initiative affecting higher education is far more likely to reflect in tone and content the values embedded in broader statewide reform agenda. The basic premise behind the move to "reinvent government" is that the public sector must be restructured in order to function efficiently and cost effectively in today's more market-oriented economy.* (Ruppert, 1998, p. 1).

Throughout the 1990s, there was a greater use of performance indicators for assessment purposes by public colleges and universities (Cave, Hanney, Henkel, and Kogan, 1997; Zumeta, 2001). States such as Missouri, Tennessee, and particularly South Carolina have been fairly aggressive in adopting certain aspects of these measures. Concurrently, there has been a shift in accrediting agencies' assessment processes as they have moved from a resources-centered assessment (emphasizing sound revenue sources, faculty credentials, and suitable facilities) to a more student-centered assessment (Astin, 1993). It also was determined during the late 1980s and early 1990s, that if performance indicators were to be effective in the decision-making process, both public officials and public institutions needed to

- Keep and expand the best of the performance indicator scheme, the willingness to examine, to enumerate where appropriate, and to expound on;
- Develop and institute regular institutional study and review (internal self-assessment and external visits) that engage professionals in the process of improving their organization and that create the needed data and opinions as well as the psychological ownership of the resulting recommendations;
- Focus on the government needs and their measures as well as the form, process, health and achievements (via goal-by-goal analysis) of individual colleges and universities and their programs (Kells, 1990).

Performance indicators for many public institutions have been broadly defined by four values: efficiency, quality, equity, and choice (Burke, 1998). For example, in 1996 the Maryland Higher Education Commission established a new accountability system that included five student-centered indicators: 1) Quality—as it is defined by how campuses can show whether they are doing a good job; 2) Effectiveness—as it is indicated when campuses can demonstrate whether students are progressing and performing well; 3) Access—as it is demonstrated whenever campuses can show whether they are accessible and are meeting the needs of students in all regions; 4) Diversity—as it is evidenced when a campus can evaluate whether students, faculty, and staff reflect the state's gender and racial make-up; and 5) Efficiency and allocation of resources—as it is manifested when campuses can determine how productively funds and facilities are being used (Maryland Higher Education Commission, Maryland, 1998).

Maryland's Commission also has placed an increased emphasis on assessing cost containment measures.

> To achieve greater standardization in the reporting of cost containment information, more precise language was added to the guidelines for the institutions' performance accountability report. As a result, nearly all of the public campuses provided detailed description and specific dollar amounts about how they reduced waste, improved the overall efficiency of their operations,

and achieved cost savings (Maryland Higher Education Commission, Maryland, 1998, p. 5).

South Carolina's performance indicators include nine areas: "mission focus; quality of faculty; instructional quality; institutional cooperation and collaboration; administrative efficiency; entrance requirements for students; graduates' achievements; "user friendliness"; and research spending (Zumeta, 2001, p. 176). Accordingly, most of South Carolina's indicators relate more to input and process (that tend to implicate costs saving and efficiencies) and less to outcome/output. For example, faculty credentials: whether faculty performance reviews follow best practices; class size; average credit hours taught by faculty, ratio of indirect to total costs; and use of best practices in the administration all relate to input and process (Zumeta, 2001). This also suggests a strong influence from the business community in South Carolina in the creation of performance indicators. The significant push for performance funding in the state of South Carolina came from the business community which felt the higher education system needed to be more responsive and cost effective (Zumeta, 2001). However, due to the potential varying results these indicators may produce on each state institution in reference to budget allocations in South Carolina, the legislators are still reviewing policy in this area. A more formal discussion on performance funding and budgeting is presented in the next section from Boatright (1995). Still, it is worth noting that many state boards and commissions of higher education include performance indicators as criteria in examining assessment and accountability and in making recommendations for effective and efficient resources management (Florida State Postsecondary Education Planning Commission, 1995; Freeman, 1994; South Carolina Commission on Higher Education, 1997).

University of Wisconsin's System Accountability
Since public universities, such as the statewide University of Wisconsin (UW) systems, are complex institutions that serve a variety of needs and audiences in many different locations, it is often difficult to tell whether or not the system is achieving the goals the public thinks are worthwhile—especially the goal of using resources

efficiently. Thus, the common perception is that such complex oper-
ations always will remain incomprehensible to members of the gen-
eral public.

The complexity of the UW system is evidenced, in part, by the
breadth, as it is composed of two doctoral granting universities, eleven
comprehensive universities, thirteen freshman-sophomore centers, and
statewide extension programs. These individual universities, centers,
and programs report to a single board of regents and are coordinated
by a central administration and a system president. Measuring the suc-
cess of such a diverse organization in ways that will be universally
meaningful is a challenge. Increasingly, UW has come to recognize that
measurement and assessment are necessary if public universities are to
demonstrate their accountability and to retain the trust and goodwill
of their many stakeholders by demonstrating that the institution indeed
is performing well.

In 1992, in response to widespread concern about the level of
compensation for the UW system faculty and academic staff and in
response to concern about the complicated process by which annual
pay increases were determined, a Governor's Commission was con-
vened. The Commission included members of the UW system
Board of Regents, legislators, state officials, corporate executives, and
UW system representatives. The commission issued a report to Gov-
ernor Tommy Thompson and presented four findings, one of which
was that "because the authority [for the process of determining pay
increases] is diffused among many parties, accountability for these
decisions also is diffused" (Compensation Commission, 1992,
p. 13). The Commission recommended "the UW System Board of
Regents should be delegated greater authority and greater account-
ability for management of its operations, including setting faculty
and academic staff compensation levels and procedures" (Compen-
sation Commission, 1992, p. 18). Another recommendation
addressed accountability in greater detail, stating that "the UW sys-
tem should be required to adopt appropriate accountability mea-
sures. The UW, at the system and/or institution level, should be held

*accountable in the following seven general areas: effectiveness, effi-
ciency, quality, access, diversity, stewardship of assets, and contributions to compelling state needs. The governor should appoint a
task force composed primarily of representatives from legislative and
executive branches, faculty and academic staff, the UW System, and
the UW Board of Regents. Other public members may be included.
The purpose of the task force is to identify specific indicators to be
utilized to measure performance in these areas" (Compensation
Commission, 1992, p. 20).*

*Six months passed before the Governor's Task Force on Univer-
sity of Wisconsin Accountability Measures was created by executive
order on March 17, 1993. In forming the task force, Governor
Thompson repeated the recommendation of the Commission report,
adding that it also was charged with assessing "the benefits and costs,
including the data collection costs, of indicators," and that "these
indicators should be utilized as the accountability measures to be
reported publicly by the UW System and upon which the UW System should be judged by Wisconsin citizens, legislators, and other
stakeholders" (Executive Order No. 177, 1993, pp. 1–2). As a
result, six recommendations were explicitly developed by the Task
Force "to establish a strengthened accountability system for the UW
System," with the expressed purpose of developing a "design to
heighten the effectiveness of the UW System and improve the public's understanding of and confidence in the UW System" (Accountability Task Force, 1993, p. 2).*

The recommendations were as follows:

1. *That the UW System Board of Regents, in consultation
   with the governor and the legislature, establish a core set of
   indicators that the Board of Regents monitors and publi-
   cizes. The Board of Regents should establish a core set of
   indicators that demonstrates the UW System's accountability in the following areas: providing a high-quality
   undergraduate education; meeting the needs of business*

*and other organizations in Wisconsin; and being consumer
oriented and responsive to customer concerns.*

2. *That a set of core indicators should be established and baseline data should be made available for each of the indicators, and that the UW Board of Regents would evaluate the
data and set performance goals related to each of the identified indicators.*

3. *That, besides being accountable for a set of indicators, the
UW System and each UW institution, under the direction,
review and approval of the Board of Regents, establishes
processes that demonstrate a commitment to accountability.*

4. *That the accountability measures be publicized in an
annual report or report card issued by the UW System and
is presented to the governor and Legislature in a highly visible manner.*

5. *That there be consequences for failing to act to meet the
accountability goals and rewards for special efforts which
lead to success in meeting goals.*

6. *That there be a process to review the suitability of the
accountability measures and take into consideration new
public reports concerning the UW system* (Boatright, 1995,
pp. 51–55).

What is most promising here, and unusual, is to have such a clear set of
goals and indicators and to call for such a public review of whether an institution has met its goals.

Performance Funding and Budgeting

The primary objectives of state higher education budgeting are to merge inten-
tions with action, to establish a direction for higher education, and to put in
place an accountability device (Jones, 1984). Most proposed budgets for state
universities contain recommendations for increases in various program-
spending levels that also have cost implications. "Mandated increases in cost

arise from changing economic conditions, threats to financial solvency or profitability, and changes in government social policy" (Waggaman, 1991, p. 37). On the other hand, costs incurred a result of promoting special workforce programs to enhance teacher preparation, increasing funding for technology use for faculty and students, or increasing spending for minority populations seeking financial and academic assistance have costs that are attached to them that may not be totally funded through state appropriations (Illinois State Board of Higher Education, 1997; New Mexico Commission on Higher Education, 1997).

Most proposed budgets for state universities contain recommendations for increases in various program-spending levels that also have cost implications.

The recognition of these costs is usually identified through one of the two most widely used budget processes in higher education: incremental or formula-based budgeting. Incremental budgeting starts with the actual base number from the previous year (revenue and expenditures) and increases or decreases that number as a result of a set of assumptions. The changes are usually minimal, focusing on what the institution needs to maintain the operation from one year to the next. During this process, institutions pay close attention to inflationary pressures such as faculty workloads or additional student services that will have an effect on the revenue needed to cover incremental expenditures. For many, this budget model appears to present one of the better opportunities for institutions to identify and control costs. However, there are two drawbacks associated with incremental budgeting: 1) limited creativity in introducing new program initiatives (versus maintaining the status quo), and 2) a lack of provision for encouragement of a strategic direction for future resources allocation. In addition, this cost-plus method could account for problems associated with controlling costs. As Simpson (1991) explains,

> *Budget presentations generally show accrual amounts for the prior year, estimated amounts for the current year, and proposed amounts for the budget year, prior to being offset by revenues and appropriations. Estimates for years beyond the budget year are included in multiyear programming. An approach to budget formation that is*

sheer folly from the standpoint of cost control is to take the experienced expenditures level for the prior period even when they are not in the total amount budgeted, and adjust them for the demands of the period ahead. Such a cost-plus approach provides an incentive to increase cost, not contain or reduce it (Simpson, 1991, pp. 122–23).

On the other hand, formula-based budgeting, used primarily in state institutions, involves the calculation of revenues and expenditures as a result of a prescribed mathematical formula. The elements contained in the formula include a set of cost and staffing assumptions (cost per credit hour, student-faculty ratios) set against specific inputs (student enrollments, credit hours) (Meisinger, 1994). From a cost-containment standpoint, one of the major problems with this budgeting process is due to the fact that the unit-cost measurement does not take into consideration the changes in marginal cost that accompany fluctuations in enrollments (Vandament, 1989). Depending on the mix between fixed and variable costs, changes in the cost structure will occur when there are changes in volume. "By utilizing marginal cost concepts, the state or institution considers the 'extra' costs associated with adding an 'extra' student (or the increment of cost savings associated with decreasing the student body by one)" (Jones, 1984, p. 76). Another problem associated with formula-based budgeting involves the allocation of funds across the board, which does not allow for adjustments to ensure correct funding levels. This budget process has been used by states for over a half a century in an effort to establish an equitable distribution of funds to their respective institutions (Ahumada, 1990). However, when funds are allocated to all existing programs, regardless of whether funding is warranted, past behavior patterns in dealing with cost issues can be repeated without measuring differences in program needs (Boutwell, 1973).

Other budgeting methods used in higher education concentrate more on cost identification and include zero-based and program budgeting. These methods have not been as popular in state higher-education circles; however, they are widely used in the corporate world. Zero-based budgeting requires programs, at the beginning of each year, to analyze and justify all costs associated with their operation in order to ensure responsible resource allocation. However, this process has not been well received among state higher-education professionals primarily because of political fallout (Folger, 1984). Zero-based budgeting calls for operating units to perform thorough program reviews each year to justify their continuation (Balderston, 1995), and these reviews often have been found to be time-consuming and subjective. This type of budgeting, if performed in higher education, may be better suited for administrative functions than for budgeting resources within academic units (Dickmeyer, 1992).

Program budgeting originated in the federal government, in the Department of Defense specifically. This budgetary process establishes a cost-benefit analysis that links planning goals to resource expenditures within organizational activities (Vandament, 1989; Dickmeyer, 1992). This process was found to be too cumbersome for higher education as each program attempted to account for all of its cost allocations. More recently, responsibility-centered budgeting is being used by a growing number of colleges and universities (both public and private). Responsibility-centered budgeting involves a corporate-style management of resources through a decentralized budgeting system. This budgeting practice requires the formulation of a clear statement of organizational principles and objectives that are matched with policies and procedures and then rewarding cost effectiveness among the various units of the institution (Whalen, 1991). As in the private sector, inefficiencies of operation are accounted for and decisions are made that work to immediately correct the cost inefficiency. The research indicates that this process works best with state systems that include large multicampus sites, because all of the sites offered incentives to augment state appropriations and are treated "as a separate financial entity with the right, privilege, and responsibility to manage [their] own funds" (Whalen, 1991, p. 7). The sites with clearly defined incentives to manage resources effectively retain outstanding balances, which they then may use at their discretion to fulfill their department goals and objectives.

In an attempt to better align budget requests with efficiency and effectiveness, and in an attempt to acknowledge the public outcry for greater accountability in higher education, more states, some through mandates and others voluntarily, are moving toward some type of performance-based budgeting that includes postformula funding (State Issues Digest, 1999). This 1990s movement, led by legislators and governors, was fueled by public, state, and federal criticism of higher education concerning the need for clearer indicators of productivity and performance (Burke, 1998). In 1997, the Nelson A. Rockefeller Institute of Government surveyed each state to inquire if they had adopted performance funding or budgeting and if not, if they planned on adopting the practice some time in the near future. In the first year, sixteen states (or 30 percent of the total states in the United States), including Colorado, Florida, Georgia, Hawaii, Idaho, Illinois, Indiana, Iowa, Kansas, Mississippi, Nebraska, North Carolina, Oklahoma, Rhode Island, Texas, and West Virginia, all reported use of performance funding and/or budgeting. The number of states using this budget practice increased to twenty-one states or 42 percent of the total in 1998 and then to twenty-three states or 46 percent of the total in 1999 (Burke, Modarresi, and Serban, 1999). Of the twenty-three states, eleven incorporated the practice as a result of mandates, and all states initiated the practice either through state coordinating boards, the legislature, or the governor's office.

It is useful to distinguish between the differences in performance budgeting versus performance funding. Performance budgeting occurs when "state government or coordinating boards [use] indirectly, reports of institutional achievements on performance indicators as a general context in shaping the total budgets for colleges and universities," whereas performance funding occurs when "special state funding [is] tied directly to the achievements of public colleges and universities on specific indicators" (Burke and Serban, 1998, p. 3).

Performance-based funding includes the following elements:

- The objectives to be attained—either outcomes or demonstrations of exemplary practice.
- The metrics of success—which involve specific measures or definitions that determine performance.
- The basis of reward—the benchmarks of success.
- The process for resource allocation (Jones, 1997).

Performance-based budgeting includes four basic characteristics:

- It presents the major purpose for which funds are allocated and sets measurable objectives.
- It reports on past performance and uses common cost classifications that allow programs to be compared rather then focusing on line comparisons.
- It offers management flexibility to reallocate money as needed and to provide rewards for achievement and penalties for failure.
- It incorporates findings from previous program evaluations that are not supported by creditable information that can be independently audited (Carter, 1994, p. 5).

Of the two, it appears that performance budgeting would contribute more information for both state policy makers and campus administrators to discover cost containment opportunities for their respective institutions.

Despite the growing popularity of this budget process, there are drawbacks. First, if states decided to allocate funding totally on a performance basis, the level of funding each year could vary, which could work to the detriment of the institution (Ashworth, 1994). Second, colleges and universities would need to make dramatic adjustments to fixed and variable cost structures in order to match the level of funding each year. These adjustments could mean the hiring of faculty and staff in years where performance is positive and massive layoffs in the following year if performance does not meet expectations. Third, an emphasis is placed on developing consensus regarding performance indicators that reflect realistic objectives and that reflect achievable outcomes (Ashworth, 1994; Nedwek, 1996). The agreement is usually between the state system policy makers (state legislatures plus coordinating boards), the institutions, and the individuals (Dochy and Segers, 1990). The state higher-education policy makers and institutions concentrate on measures of effectiveness, efficiency, and economy (Sizer, 1989). "Indicators of effectiveness are concerned with goal attainment, efficiency with unit costs for goal attainment, and economy with ways to reduce costs while achieving goals and objectives" (Nedwek, 1996, p. 63). This would indicate that state policy makers might be leaning toward budget processes that promote a better understanding of cost containment relationships with their respective institutions. Again, such budget processes also would indicate a need for policy makers to possess more of a sophisticated understanding of the relationship between additional revenues and incremental costs. It is worth noting that the primary purpose for performance funding was not cost containment. Performance funding replaced previous formula funding methods in an effort to better respond to changes in public policy as such changes influenced accountability and productivity (Serban, 1998). Thus, whether performance budgeting adequately promotes greater cost efficiency is still being investigated.

As such budget practices are more widely considered, implemented, and more widely scrutinized, attention to the allocation of state resources and the responsiveness of budget performance funding is burgeoning (State Issues Digest, 1999). Nonetheless, this process is not without its growing pains and not without unforeseen or indirect consequences on cost containment. According to a general consensus, "as the 1990s came to a close, the experience with performance-based budgeting was disappointing to those who believed that outcomes, not inputs, should determine the state funding priorities. Fewer than a dozen states have adopted performance-based systems, setting aside a small share of higher education funding into special funds allocated based on performance measures. Few states have built performance into their basic funding formula" (Hauptman, 2001, p. 67).

The following performance-funding vignette featuring the state of Kentucky further explains issues associated with implementing performance-based funding programs while attempting to balance state and campus interest. The Kentucky vignette presents a situation where gaining consensus and continuity in the budgeting process is essential. The performance funding initiative attempted in Kentucky leaves us troubled by the following questions and by the ongoing problems implied therein. How can leaders of campus and coordinating boards reach a collegial consensus on a performance program that satisfies both collective accountability and institutional diversity? How can performance funding championed by one governor survive under a successor?

Kentucky

At Kentucky University, the implementation of performance funding demonstrated the classic conflict between coordinating agencies who were pushing for greater accountability and university presidents who were striving to protect institutional autonomy. Balancing state and campus interests constitutes the critical issue in performance funding and often can result in tension and conflicts. Clashes between the coordinating agencies and the university president arose during the deliberation of the Jones's Commission and erupted repeatedly during the two-year struggle to develop a permanent plan for performance funding. Two questions dominated the debate: should the indicators be mandated or should they be largely discretionary for institutions, and should campuses have wide choice or restricted choice in indicator weights? The Jones's Commission recommended common indicators, with the campus choice of indicator weights in adopting five performance areas that stressed student persistence, student and employer satisfaction, research and service productivity, and management efficiency. The Commission also developed twenty-six indicators that were specific, quantifiable, and mostly output and outcome measures drawn from the accountability reports required for public colleges and universities (Governor's Commission, 1993). Although the campus presidents fought for more discretion regarding the indicators, weights, and standards, to eighteen million in new money for performance funding in the 1995-96 budget they agreed to a more restrictive (and possibly temporary) budget plan.

The final plan adopted by Council on Higher Education (CHE) in July 1996 reflected the compromise reached to resolve the conflicts. Early on, the CHE agreed that two-thirds of any new state appropriation (up to a 3-percent increase) would fund current activities and services. The remainder would be split 60 percent to account for equity and just 40 percent to account for performance. Moreover, a budget cut for higher education would automatically suspend performance funding. The final plan contained four common and eight voluntary indicators, including up to two institution-specific items. The plan included that the proviso campuses could assign weights within a prescribed range, as long as the prescribed indicators received at least 50 percent of the total points. In addition, the plan provided for a means of phasing in formula funding. For example, during the first two biennia, the plan rewarded campuses for introducing the process for implementing the indicators; the reward of results came only in the third biennia.

The consultation process dramatically altered the proposal for performance funding in the Commission's report. Even those precise measures that did not remain in the final program, such as retention and graduation rates, were made more variable in that campuses were allowed to use one or both of these indicators to measure their performance. The final plan showed a decided shift from output and outcome to process measures. The Commission's plan had proposed funding improved results and considered evidence of actions taken and processes adopted during the initial round of performance funding when baseline data was not as readily available. The conflict between state interest and campus interest did produce some interesting innovations, in particular, the inclusion of campus-specific indicators and ranges for indicator rates. If the Commission's proposal leaned toward statewide accountability, the final plan tilted toward campus diversity. In the end, both lacked the balance required to maintain the support of both state and campus leaders.

Whatever the merits of the final plan, according to many, it had taken too long to achieve and had created too much conflict in the process. Legislators wondered why there had been so much fuss when so little money was involved: only $3.3 million allocated for 1996-97 for performance funding and $2.6 million allocated for 1997-98. The Task Force on Higher Education fully registered the legislature's disappointment with the process and the product, bluntly declaring that "efforts to implement a meaningful system of performance funding [had] been ineffective" (Kentucky General Assembly, 1996). In any case, the newly elected governor, Governor Patton, had already decided on a new and different agenda. He hoped to transform the governance and goals of higher education through incentive funding, which would provide up-front money to encourage compliance, rather than by funding for results (Patton, 1997). The general assembly passed the plan at an extraordinary session (House Bills 1 and 4, Special Sessions, Kentucky, May 30 and 27, 1997) and thus effectively ended any efforts to use performance funding.

The Kentucky story exposes the perennial problems of trying to gain consensus and trying to ensure continuity. The funding initiative attempted in Kentucky demonstrates the difficulties inherent in calling upon leaders of campus and coordinating boards to reach a collegial consensus on a performance program that satisfies both collective accountability and institutional diversity.

Moreover, the story of what occurred in Kentucky also demonstrates the difficulty in adopting and implementing a specific form of funding when one's successor may call for another form of budgeting during his or her tenure (Burke and Serban, 1998).

Outside of the performance-funding sphere, Indiana University switched to responsibility-centered budgeting to control costs in an environment of reduced state support. During this effort, it developed an economic model that provided it with essential cost information on its inputs.

The Indiana University Experience

Like its peers in higher education, Indiana University is facing the challenge of increasing costs coupled with diminishing state support. As a result, Indiana recently implemented responsibility-centered management (RCM), which gave deans the authority to collect and distribute their own financial resources. The approach came with the caveat that the deans needed to know how the distribution of resources could best be accomplished, and in particular, where resources could best be recovered and then where they could best be reallocated. These budgeting processes also required the dean to portray the cost of inputs, such as personnel, rather than the cost of outputs, such as large degree programs. It was believed that such a concentration on inputs would encourage administrators to become more aware of the fundamental disconnection between how academic administrators think about the future in terms of outputs and costs. (DeHayes and Lovrinic, 1994)

Responsibility-centered management came with the caveat that the deans needed to know how the distribution of resources could best be accomplished.

Once this allocation of resources was delegated to operational levels, it became clear that it was necessary for resource managers to fully understand the cost of their operations and the impact of their reallocation decisions. Initial steps in defining the theory of the model began in January 1991. And soon thereafter the Indiana University-Purdue University Indianapolis (IUPUI) campus, one of eight in the Indiana University system, volunteered to be the prototype site for the new efficiency effort. A team drawn from the schools of dentistry and business, together with the campus accounting office, met with an internal consulting group to develop economic models for two of the outputs of the Indianapolis campus outputs: the Bachelors of Science degree in business and the graduate degree of Doctorate of Dental Sciences in Dentistry (DeHayes and Lovrinic, 1994).

IUPUI proved to be particularly receptive to both the implementation of RCM and the development of economic modeling. A comparatively new campus (in existence since, 1969), it has more than 27,000 students and 1,400 full-time faculty and offers diverse degree programs in nineteen schools. IUPUI is a joint venture between Indiana University and Purdue University, with Indiana University serving as the manager partner. The collaboration between the two universities is distinctive as IUPUI is helping to define a new type of American urban university that excels in research (IUPUI generated nearly $90 million in external support in 1992-93) while offering a full range of educational programs from associates degrees and college preparatory study to professional and doctoral degrees (DeHayes and Lovrinic, 1994).

Using activity-based costing techniques, the IUPUI team developed and defined the basic mechanics of the model. As a result of their efforts, a range of tools were created for analyzing the current operation and limiting future costs. The campus leadership decided to expand and broaden the model effort incrementally over the years (DeHayes and Lovrinic, 1994).

The economic model that the IUPUI team developed consists of the following elements:

- A graphic view of the interrelated organizations that depicts the outputs produced by academic units and the services produced by support units that are then consumed by academic units.
- An activity-based costing matrix that defines the costs of various outputs and allows "what-if" cost analyses in response to various input parameters.
- Workflow analyses that can assist the organization in enhancing its current activities through a detailed review and reengineering of the tasks involved in those activities (DeHayes and Lovrinic, 1994).

The model has helped deans and directors optimize their resource allocation decisions because it helps them to more clearly understand the costs associated with operations. The model can also be a key component in successfully realizing the benefits of RCM as it helps to demonstrate how resources can be reallocated during periods of constrained funding (DeHayes and Lovrinic, 1994).

In short, the model enables units to determine more accurate cost-performance measures for costing the unit's products, for identifying restructuring opportunities, and for estimating the impact of proposed changes in operations and varying customer demand. In addition, the model has four peripheral benefits: "development of a collective understanding of how each unit contributes to the outputs of the campus (instruction, research, and service: a more precise illustration of the interdependencies among units in the fulfillment of their missions; a broader management understanding of unit-level operations; and the establishment of a foundation for reengineering operations and applying total quality management through development of costing benchmarks for continuous improvement efforts" (DeHayes and Lovrinic, 1994, p. 84).

Restructuring

In the corporate sector, restructuring is characterized by a reallocation or selling off of assets to support changes in market strategy. Restructuring initiatives usually are introduced as result of stagnating sales and weak earnings performance prompted by a loss in market share (Hammer and Champy, 1993; Handy, 1994). Other conditions that may make restructuring necessary are made apparent in the corporate sector when the performance of vital business units decline as a result of weak market conditions; when technology changes in the industry occur that create competitive disadvantages; and when new leadership wants to take the corporation in a new direction (Thompson and Strickland, 1995).

Some restructuring strategies for large corporations include selling off business units, replacing senior level executives, decreasing debt to increase cash flow opportunities, employing strategic capital expenditures, and implementing significant changes in the general workforce (such as layoffs and firings) to match new organizational objectives. For example, in 1992, Sears, Roebuck and Co. abandoned its financial supermarket strategy in the last quarter of 1992. Directors approved a program to spin off Sears, Dean Witter Financial Services Group, most of its Caldwell Banker real-estate holdings, and 20 percent of its Allstate insurance unit. Furthermore, in the first quarter of 1993, Sears closed its catalog business (its core business) again, reversing the strategy formulated in 1981. Thus, Edward Brennan, chairman of Sears, abandoned his dream of developing a financial service supermarket. Sears has steadily lost market share in retailing, dropping from the number one to the number three position behind discounters Wal-Mart Stores Inc. and Kmart Corp. (Hitt, Ireland, and Hoskisson, 1995).

For restructuring to be successful in the private sector, companies have relied upon shifting into areas of business where there are clear competitive advantages that produce gains in productivity and innovation (Filippello, 1999). The emphasis lies not only on the reduction of cost structure, but also on long-term revenue growth. Some of the more well-known strategies incorporated in successful corporate restructuring ventures include what was done at Scott Paper in 1996.

1. *Form the right management team.* Poorly performing executives were fired, including 70 percent of upper management in the first year alone. New executives who had strong track records were brought in only as needed. In addition, Dunlap, the chief executive officer, hired fourteen experienced marketing directors from Kimberly-Clark, Procter & Gamble, Colgate-Palmolive, and Coca-Cola. As a result of such sweeping changes, he developed a small inner circle of trusted executives with diverse skills and personalities.

2. *Cut costs.* As a result of cutting 11,200 jobs, payroll was reduced by 35 percent. Procurement was consolidated on a worldwide basis. The items stocked in inventories were reduced from 11,000 to 2,000. Executive perks (such as jets, cars, and beach houses) were eliminated. The lavish corporate headquarters were sold and alternative space was rented. Dunlap followed the principle of doing in-house only what was perceived to

give the company a competitive advantage, and thus the company outsourced many functions (Weston, Jawien, and Levitas, 1998).

3. *Focus on core business.* Unrelated businesses, such as health care, food service, and a cogeneration power plant, were sold. In addition, Scott sold $2 billion in non-core assets within the first year. Dunlap focused on high-growth products within the core business, selling off the coated paper activity for $1.6 billion (Weston, Jawien, and Levitas, 1998).

4. *Develop a strategy.* The product line was pared down. Dunlap eliminated 31 percent of the procurement product items offered. Testing the "Rule of 55" showed that 50 percent of the products produced only 5 percent of the company's revenue and earning. So more than 500 domestic warehouses reduced the number of products from seventy to ten. The remaining products were reduced by sales growth of 24.5 percent and operating margins of 20.4 percent. Marketing efforts were refocused around a universal product line, with the slogan, "Scott the world over." (Weston, Jawien, and Levitas, 1998, p. 2). This saved millions in advertising and promotional expense. Finally, stock awards were not granted unless performance targets were met.

Then, in July 1995, Kimberly-Clark purchased Scott Paper and during the restructuring period, Scott Paper's market value increased by $6.5 billion.

In higher education, restructuring initiatives are similar in that they are characterized by targeted sweeping cutbacks at the institutional level primarily as a result of weak financial performance. (El-Khawas, 1994; Matthews and Curry, 1995). More recently, the restructuring of the state role in higher education was also meant to restore public confidence in the system (MacTaggart, 1996). Because policy makers at the state level are unable to control costs directly at the institutional level, they must influence cost factors through the control of the governance system (Novak, 1996). Unlike the corporate sector, restructuring in state higher education has to contend internally with decisions by consensus, traditional environmental resistances to change, and a stoic attitude from faculty even during difficult financial periods (Breneman, 1994). In addition, if the trend in modern corporate America tends toward decentralization of control to enhance operating efficiencies, then state higher education appears to be moving in the opposite direction with its emphasis upon the centralization of governance structures (Novak, 1996). The uneasiness expressed by the general public (and even by members of the business sector) over increasing tuition costs and limited access to higher education has led to conversations concerning restructuring. In 1994, the New Jersey education system was reorganized when the Higher Education Restructuring Act abolished cumbersome state oversight with the goal of improving accountability at the institutional level. It was hoped that this act would spawn creativity and innovation in meeting the mission that feeds into statewide goals and objectives (New Jersey Commission on Higher Education, 1999). The New Jersey initiative produced bond proposals totaling $550 million for capital improvements at four-year institutions and an enactment of a $55 million higher education technology fund.

During the economic downturn in the early 1990s, many state coordinating boards of higher education had the authority to make unilateral decisions that impacted the cost structure. Some of those decisions included such acts as the elimination of excessive doctoral and undergraduate programs as well as the closing of campus sites that had become too costly to operate (Benjamin and Carrol, 1993). Other initiatives prompted by restructuring have included reductions in administrative staffs, deferring maintenance, dropping or merging programs, and freezing salaries (El-Khawas, 1994; Nicklin, 1996). States such as North Dakota, Massachusetts, Alaska, Minnesota, and Maryland all demonstrated their commitment to cost containment through such actions (MacTaggart, 1996). However, many of the decisions made by the coordination boards during the early 1990s came primarily as a result of mandated budget cuts by the state as opposed to restructuring initiatives that contained cost containment strategies.

At the state institutional level, questions concerning limited resources, escalating costs, access, and quality have provoked concern about the current structure of colleges and universities and their ability to get the job done (Benjamin and Carrol, 1993). Initial responses in the 1990s from higher education administrators mirrored the corporate response of concentrating on downsizing or on addressing quality control problems. "Short-term responses often involve slashing expenditures. Common retrenchment practices include hiring freezes and pay cuts, cutbacks in merit-based student aid, reductions in routine maintenance, cutbacks in research funding, and reductions in student services" (Myers, 1996, p. 69). However, such acts may not, in the end, constitute effective long-term strategies; therefore, retrenchment should be replaced by restructuring. Restructuring replaces retrenchment's reliance "on an ethos of crisis management" by encouraging a "reliance on the tenets of strategic planning, mission reaffirmation, environmental scanning, goal formation, and evaluation and revision" (Myers, 1996, p. 70). Accordingly, restructuring in its truest form at the institutional level should employ directional change in the way a college or university conducts business. Complete restructuring ultimately would involve the reshaping of the total organization, including how pedagogy and curriculum are conceived and conducted (Naylor and Willimon, 1997).

In times of retrenchment, even when universities are looking for a quick fix to specific financial problems, restructuring does attempt to require strategic planning whereby the vision and mission of the institution are revisited (Myers, 1996). Prompted by the state to plan more strategically, some universities also have engaged in administrative and academic restructuring initiatives which include increasing the use of technology to improve teaching and learning (Taylor and Massy, 1996; Massy, 1996). However, this process of restructuring can be complicated and costly if state policy makers (legislature and governors) and institutions do not agree on the overall mission and goals of the university. For example,

> *when the California State University faced significant fiscal cuts in 1992, three campuses, each with the same core mission (teaching undergraduates), proposed radically different responses. One proposed the elimination of nine departments whose absence would not prevent the college from meeting its core mission. A second proposal involved cutting the entire library acquisition budget, although some level of acquisition would seem literally indispensable. The third campus proposed to eliminate all part-time faculty—its busiest and most cost effective teachers. The dramatic differences between the three proposals strongly suggest that each*

*college either had a very different sense of the mission it was sup-
posed to serve or a very different set of internal priorities within
that mission* (Benjamin and Carrol, 1993, pp. 3–4).

At other times, restructuring decisions at the state higher education level
can serve their purpose by matching goals and objectives with positive changes
in efficiency and productivity. In the early 1990s, institutions in the state
of Virginia responded to a report from the "Commission on the University of
the 21st Century," by pledging

- To continue efforts to become more efficient but not at the expense of
  becoming less effective;
- To consider strategies in which the organization and administration of colleges and universities could be made less costly;
- To utilize technology where it would increase faculty productivity, despite
  being under budget constraints;
- To realize there are different costs associated with how curriculums are orga-
  nized, particularly given that institutions are reviewing the entire curriculum with an eye toward making it more efficient (Virginia Higher
  Education, 1991).

In 1995, the Board of Regents for the Montana University System put forth
a restructuring plan with emphasis on outcomes that featured some of the following initiatives, each of which carries financial implications:

- The elimination of remedial education at four-year institutions and the provision that students will pay full cost (state-support level plus tuition) for
  any remedial work taken within the Montana University System.
- Shortened time to degree by focusing on the front end of the entry
  process and on the high school-postsecondary transition, and by emphasizing advanced placement, tech prep, and other programs that meld secondary and postsecondary schooling.
- High budget priority given to technology and faculty and staff development
  with a stated percentage of each year's operating budget designated for and

then invested in upgrading the skills of faculty and staff. Emphasis also should be placed on improving teaching effectiveness and instructional technology.

- Major initiatives to address the efficiency of administrative services. Recommendations will include, but not to be limited to, purchasing, contracting, liability insurance, auditing, facilities management, personal administration, financial aid services, and technologies management. Private-sector incentives and business will be adopted wherever appropriate. Benchmarking will be used where applicable. The goal should be to review operations and to identify those activities that can be provided more efficiently by privatizing.

- Productivity gains should result in savings that offset both the rising cost of education and the reduction in state support; to that end, the university should develop a plan to reinvest in higher education. Such incentives and investments are the building blocks of future efficiency and effectiveness. Agreements should ensure that savings from productivity are shared between the state and higher education and also with higher education managers at all levels. In other words, an incentive structure is needed that encourages managers to find ways to do business. Skimming all savings from the top and simply reducing financial commitments by an equal amount are counterproductive to long-term sustainability. Savings provide the funding sources for future investment and ensure that future productivity increases. Business logic that links savings and investment is the model's most fundamental ingredient as it is necessary in order for the productivity-savings-investment-productivity cycle to succeed (Board of Regents Resolution, The Restructuring of the Montana University System Phase Two, 1995).

An incentive structure is needed that encourages managers to find ways to do business.

Almost twenty years ago, the state of Alaska developed a restructuring plan to cope with a serious loss in revenues due in part to declines in oil prices. However, this presented the Boards of Regents an opportunity to develop a plan (presented in the following from Gaylord and Rogers, 1988) that would enhance the quality education while remaining within an affordable economic structure.

Restructuring the University of Alaska Statewide System of Higher Education

As a result of dramatic reductions in state revenues (due to the 1984-85 collapses in world oil prices), the state of Alaska had to restructure its entire higher education system. It became obvious that the only way to accommodate the magnitude of the budget reductions meant radically changing the structure of the system. The strategy involved inviting various internal and external constituencies to assist in formulating restructuring alternatives. The two major constraints mandated by the Boards of Regents included 1) a system reduction plan that had to meet the budget reduction targets, and, at the same time, had to provide the highest possible level of service in terms of the programs and courses offered, and 2) the system restructuring plan had to meet the budget reduction targets, but at the same time it had to attempt to provide the highest level of access in terms of providing courses and programs at the current educational delivery sites. Three major restructuring alternatives were considered: 1) a single accrediting university in the state with one president 2) a single multi-campus community college, three accredited universities, and a reduced central office administration, and 3) three accredited universities, no accredited community colleges, and a reduced central office of administration.

Foremost in its accomplishments, the restructuring plan met the primary goal of creating a university system that provided essentially the same level of academic opportunities for the residents of the state while considerably reducing the complexity and cost of the delivery system. Additional positive outcomes included a much-improved process of students transferring between institutions, a simplified course numbering scheme, and bringing together faculty who had been in a more isolated educational environment to form a more critical mass. Possible negative outcomes, which could prove to be significant, included the effects on staff morale, legal challenges, labor relation problems, and a desire to separate community colleges from the university (Gaylord and Rogers, 1988, p. 18).

Summary

The financial health of state institutions in higher education is contingent upon the economic well-being of the states where they preside. While most states have been experiencing solid economic growth as a result of a robust economy, institutions still have to compete for their share of revenue with other sectors. Moreover, while states' citizens have become wealthier, the portion of personal income allocated to higher education has declined. Evidence shows that from academic year 1990-91 to academic year 1999-2000, overall state higher education appropriations per $1,000 of personal income fell from $39 to $8. During this period, only two states—Arkansas and Mississippi—posted increases in this measure.

The best relationships between state policy makers for higher education and higher education institutions have been those that try to regard the decision-making process as a joint venture. However, state policy makers for higher education may not always be cognizant of whether their actions contribute to cost containment at the institutional level or act as barriers that create less opportunity for these institutions to reduce cost.

Assessment and accountability in state four-year institutions has been of paramount importance to lawmakers, state executives, and the general public. Assessment, by and large, relies upon evaluations of students and program performance rather than the current reputation of the institution. Accountability, on the other hand, deals with the allocation of resources to those programs that experience positive outcomes in relationship to specific goals set by the institution or set by external bodies. Over the last

The best relationships between state policy makers for higher education and higher education institutions have been those that try to regard the decision-making process as a joint venture.

ten years, there has been a greater use of performance indicators by colleges and universities in assessment and accountability models. Such performance indicators have been defined by four basic values: efficiency, quality, equity, and choice. Many state boards of higher education include performance indicators as criteria in examining assessment and accountability recommendations for effective and efficient resource management which should ultimately lead to cost containment opportunities.

In an attempt to better align budget requests with efficiency and effectiveness, and to acknowledge the public outcry for greater accountability in higher education, more states, some through mandates and others voluntarily, are moving toward some type of performance-based budgeting that includes post-formula funding. There has been some confusion over the difference in performance budgeting versus performance funding. Performance budgeting concentrates on the use of performance indicators as a tool for the state coordination board to construct college and university budgets. Performance funding is tied directly to the achievements of public colleges and universities and is based on specific indicators. There are political arguments for and against both budget processes, but cost containment issues play a large roll in any budget plan or model.

Restructuring initiatives in higher education at the state institutional level have been characterized by targeted, yet sweeping, cutbacks primarily as a means of correcting poor financial performance. However, recently, restructuring has also affected the role the state plays in higher education. In an effort to restore public confidence during the economic downturn period of the early 1990s, many state coordinating boards of higher education had the authority to make unilateral decisions that impacted the cost structure. Some of those decisions included the elimination of excessive doctoral and undergraduate programs as well as closing down campus sites that had been too costly to operate.

Conclusion and Recommendations

Summary of Chapter Issues (Were the Questions Answered?)

In response to questions posed in this issue on cost containment, we put forward specific observations from the literature that may be significant for university administrators and academic program planners. In "What's Driving Your Instructional Cost?" we posed the question, What is driving instructional cost, that represents, on average, approximately 30 percent of total expenditures for public and private four-year institutions? Although average salaries for full-time faculty have been increasing above the annual inflation rate and remain the primary portion of instructional cost, benefits cost (health care and retirement) have been increasing well above the consumer price index and are expected to continue in an upward spiral. Ironically, the increased use of adjunct faculty was deemed a cost savings opportunity for most academic departments. However, with the possibility of formulating collective bargaining for adjunct faculty, this could substantially increase instructional cost for the future.

The productivity argument is centered on two basic issues: 1) faculty view productivity as relating more to how much they are able to generate in the area of journal publications and the amount of funds the university can count on from the number of sponsored research grants, whereas 2) college and university administrators equate faculty productivity primarily with the number of teaching loads and academic advising of students. Studies have found that full-time faculty who possess active research agendas are paid higher salaries than those who concentrate on their activities in the classroom. Most of the recommendations that relate to cost containment under productivity, particularly at state four-year institutions, cite that faculty should spend more time in the classroom teaching larger classes. The instruction of large classes did raise issues of quality. However, the savings in instructional cost in the long run outweighed most concerns in this area. Also suggested was an increase in the use of instructional technology.

The private sector (business community) and some state legislators have questioned their respective institutions' commitment to tenure, principally because of tenure's financial designation as a fixed cost. Faculty who are tenured leave college and university administrators with limited flexibility when student enrollment forecasts vary. Faculty feel that this status is warranted and any restrictions in this area would result in an attack on academic freedom. There were several recommendations presented that addressed tenure options that would have some impact on cost containment. One recommendation was to alter the ratio between tenured faculty and less expensive contract faculty. This suggests that contract faculty may be attached to a specific program revenue stream. Consequently, when funding is unavailable because of low enrollments, administrators have more flexibility in eliminating contractual faculty positions. A second recommendation was to increase options on tenure contracts that would allow more financial incentives tied to performance in return for a negotiated limited scope of tenure.

In "Are There Cost Savings in Academic Libraries?" we posed the question, Are there any cost savings opportunities in academic support services, specifically academic libraries? The literature revealed that academic libraries have been quite aggressive and strategic in responding to cost containment issues for their operation. This is primarily a result of academic libraries receiving a steadily decreasing percentage of college and university operating budgets over the past years. Concurrently, library administrators have been forced to contend with rising costs in acquisitions while being challenged by students and the administration to purchase the latest in technology for operations and access to information. However, the purchase and use of technology has actually benefited academic libraries in relationship to cost containment. For example individual workstations (desktop computers) that are connected to client-server networks have replaced the more expensive mainframe systems that traditionally store data. In addition, library administrators have also utilized outsourcing activities to enhance productivity and remain within tight budget allocations. One of the major efficiencies from outsourcing library services comes from catalog operations. This library function is time-consuming and requires trained staff to complete the task. Other outsourcing strategies of library services included copying activities. As an addendum, some library directors feel that the department should report to the vice president for technology as opposed to academic affairs. Through this reporting structure, library directors feel that their interests would be better served.

In "Can Plant Operations and Facilities Continue to Be Ignored?" plant operations and facilities literature suggested that colleges and universities have acknowledged deferred maintenance and more recently energy management as possible risks to cost containment. The build up of deferred maintenance over the years has come to represent the absence of astute financial management in higher education. In an effort to save and therefore allocate funds to other parts of annual operating budgets, university administrators ignored important repair and maintenance projects. From a 1995 study, it would take approximately $26 billion to seriously reduce the build up of deferred maintenance at American colleges and universities. This has produced an immediate financial and legal liability for these institutions when emergency repairs are needed. More recently, a number of specific recommendations have been made in the literature that address this financial concern. Three of the major recommendations are 1) Develop a separate fund for facilities and maintenance that would equal 2 percent of the total operating budget. This fund could be deployed immediately for current repair and maintenance, and any surplus could be rolled over to the following year's operating budget for plant operations. 2) In planning for physical plant purchases, create a fund through the separate capital budget that would fund replacement and repairs at replacement value. 3) Provide a strategic plan for facility planning to identify long-term risks and opportunities that could effect the operation of the physical plant.

4) Model the private sector by developing a facilities portfolio that would establish basic data on all campus facilities and then review the information for short-term and long-term maintenance and replacement needs. From this information, create a decision-support model that would provide financial options for funding projects. This information can then be reported to administrative decision makers who would evaluate these options as they related to the mission of the institution.

Energy management could have the most current and long-term effect on cost containment in higher education. University managers of the physical plants have paid close attention to energy cost fluctuations since the oil embargo in the late 1970s. Electricity costs represent the second highest operating expense for many institutions. Most recently, the literature identified federal and state legislation to deregulate utility companies as an opportunity for commercial and retail customers to reduce their utility cost. In theory, the average utility bill would eventually decline as a result of increased competition from the entry of new firms in the marketplace. However, the actual experience from utility deregulation in California during 2000-01 has caused concern in many other states that are close to implementing their own plans. California's problem with utility deregulation stems from a dated infrastructure, bad timing of sharp increases in oil prices, and unresolved policy questions in the deregulation plan. This produced dramatic increases in the average consumer and commercial utility bills and mandatory widespread brownouts throughout the state. Overall, it was generally recommended that colleges and universities should develop energy management plans to determine infrastructure needs and financing options, to track performance of utilities based on standards, and to develop policies for electricity usage. In addition, the use of technology in energy management was demonstrated through the vignettes presented in the chapter. The use of computers was suggested as a means of regulating electricity usage in both old and new campus buildings. As with most nonrevenue departments that need a high level of university funds to operate, planning for energy consumption should reflect the overall mission of the institution.

Energy management could have the most current and long-term effect on cost containment in higher education.

The use of outsourcing as a cost containment option has been a long-standing strategy utilized by most college and university plant operations administrators. By definition, outsourcing used in this area addressed specific cost savings benefits through the use of human resources, services, and technology. However, peripheral issues that could threaten the use of outsourcing as a cost containment strategy in this area involve the reactions from permanent university employees on contracting out jobs they have skills in, and the control of job quality and consistency by plant administrators. Consequently, it was recommended that in considering outsourcing projects for plant operations, plant administrators should determine if the same savings could be achieved through the current mix of permanent employees. If the financial decision to outsource is made, there should be an attempt to balance both interests. As an example, work projects in plant operations that involve the use of highly technical skills that are not in-house, such as heating and ventilation, could be outsourced, whereas more basic services such as housekeeping and grounds upkeep could remain in-house. The vignettes presented in this section also outlined an additional issue that could increase the cost of future operations of physical plants. The University of Pennsylvania highlighted the problem with low wages earned by workers who perform menial jobs in this area. These issues can present financial and legal challenges to institutions. More recently, Harvard University was the scene of student and minimum-wage worker protests. The groups felt that the university was wealthy enough to provide higher wages to support the minimum wage workers.

"Is Research a Facilitator or Barrier to Cost Containment?" described the many issues surrounding whether research is a facilitator or a barrier to cost containment. It emphasized that cost containment efforts significantly influence the extent to which faculty are able to conduct academic research. Because providing incentives for research activity, supporting research facilities (including equipment, instrumentation, libraries, and the collection and dissemination of information), and allocating funds for both applied and basic research are costly, each institution of higher learning must evaluate the role research can and should play in its mission.

In "Can University Student Services Remain Viable with an Increasing Cost Structure?" the authors posed the question: How can student services remain viable in the face of an increasing cost structure? As institutional costs escalate, there is a corresponding increase in the demand for financial aid. For student services administrators, there is a requirement that they not only attract students to their respective colleges, but that they also ensure those students are able to pay for their education once they are admitted. In addition, a growing concern for student services professionals operating in an environment of budget constraints has been the declining level of preparedness on the part of incoming students. This lack of preparedness not only has led to an easing of expectations and standards for entering students, but also to greater strains on student services' budgets as this sector of the university is called upon to deliver remedial instruction. We found that in order to attract students to their campuses try offering enhanced student services, many universities and colleges have investigated and implemented creative collaborative cost-saving efforts as well as privatizing or outsourcing services to reduce personnel, service delivery, and equipment costs.

In "External Cost Factors" the authors attempted to determine through the literature whether states, through specific higher-education policies, acted as facilitators or barriers to cost containment in their respective four-year institutions. The policies highlighted were assessment and accountability, performance funding and budgeting, and restructuring initiatives. Assessment is characterized as an evaluation of student and program performance, while accountability is the allocation of resources to those programs that meet specific objectives set by state higher-education governing boards. Over the last ten years, performance indicators have been used for assessment purposes at the institutional level in an effort to satisfy state policy makers. Four values—efficiency, quality, equity, and choice—have defined these indicators. The efficiency performance indicator relates more to efforts or recognition of cost measurers by attempting to measure how productive funds and facilities are. In addition, Maryland's Higher Education Commission has placed increased emphasis on cost containment measures by requesting specific information on efficiency improvements, waste reduction, and other measures to achieve cost savings. Other state boards of higher education have been following these initiatives, which suggest examples of how states facilitate cost containment in their respective public institutions.

Under performance funding and budgeting, assessment and accountability efforts were taken a step further. Budgeting for state higher education institutions has been used as an instrument to provide direction and match educational objectives with financial resources. More recently, through responsibility-centered budgeting, academic departments are required to operate more from a business model where each college has control over the inflow of revenue and outflow of expenses. This budgeting model encourages academic departments to become more cognizant of cost containment issues because the penalties for overspending and inefficiency are forced reductions in operating expenses. Under performance funding and budgeting, state coordinating boards wanted to go a step further in creating an atmosphere of accountability for their institutions. Performance-based funding is based on the demonstration of meeting set objectives, while performance-based budgeting concentrates on the major purpose for funds to be allocated. However, neither policy contains elements which pertain to cost containment opportunities. The vignettes of two states engaged in this process pointed to more attention being paid to issues associated with attempting to balance the differences in state and campus interest and arguing over how much of annual college and university budgets should be allocated based on performance. However, it was recommended that when formulating policy for both methods, state policy makers should pay closer attention to the relationship between addition revenues and incremental costs. This suggests that state policy did not act as a barrier to cost containment but it was not a high enough priority to be highlighted in the goals and objectives of performance funding and budgeting initiatives. Restructuring in both the public and privates sectors is undertaken to respond to a repositioning in the marketplace as a result of weak sales and declining enrollments. The primary strategy engaged in this process is to dramatically reduce cost to reduce a loss, or in the situation in the public sector, to match revenues. Restructuring initiatives in higher education were highlighted in the early 1990s during an economic downturn when state coordinating boards were forced to mandate the elimination of programs exacted by legislative budget cuts. This period presented opportunities for institutions of higher education, as well as corporations, to reexamine objectives and to create positive changes in efficiencies and productivity. Highlighted in the vignettes, restructuring plans included both creating a stronger institution to meet student needs for a viable academic program and improving on revenue generation and efficiencies for economic stability. In this situation, of course, states are forced to become facilitators of cost containment.

Final Comments

As Edward Shils argues:

> [u]*niversities cost immense sums of money; their achievements cannot be measured in any clear and reliable way; many persons fail in them; and they certainly do not accomplish the solution of economic and social problems which some expect of them. Nevertheless, these societies cling to them. The universities do not survive simply because professors have a vested interest in their survival . . . That would never be enough. These societies cling to them because, in the last analysis, they are their best hope for a transfigured existence* (qtd. in Casper, 1995).

While societies cling to the university's power to transfigure our existence, societies also demand that colleges and universities justify their costs. According to the College Board, "despite record enrollments and surging endowments," college tuition and fees rose 4.4 percent at four-year public institutions and 5.2 percent at four-year private institutions in 1999 (Brownstein, 2000). Furthermore, according to the College Board, "the average aid per full-time student has increased 79 percent in the last twenty years, tuition and fees have more than doubled and family income has risen an average of just 20 percent. Loans now represent 59 percent of all aid, compared with 41 percent in 1980" (Brownstein, 2000). Given such increases in both tuition and financial aid, the call to justify costs has become increasingly adamant.

Our review of the literature has made it clear that more empirical research is needed to best evaluate the actual experiences of individual institutions and the best practices those institutions have developed and implemented to encourage greater cost efficiency. Perhaps it is due to the discretion institutions of higher learning practice concerning revealing internal information regarding their finances and operations. Perhaps it is due as well to a lack of venues for publication. Nonetheless, it is clear from our research efforts that a great deal could be gained were there more widely publicized discussions of the actual practice(s) of containing costs at specific institutions. While we found the various reports and case studies that addressed financing higher education both engaging and informative, in the end, we were not always in a position to determine how successful various efforts had been as there were no long-term, quantitative (as well as qualitative) studies conducted that confirmed whether the efforts to contain costs had achieved their objectives and whether these efforts could be duplicated productively at other colleges and universities.

Second, more research needs to be done to ascertain whether external bodies—such as government agencies—can best assess the cost efficiency of four-year colleges and universities. This concern applies most specifically to state colleges and universities; however, external bodies have an impact on private institutions as well. State higher education coordinating boards and agencies, state legislators, and governors have recently exhibited a strong propensity for front-line involvement with their respective institutions in academic and financial decisions once reserved exclusively for leadership at the institutional level. Assessment methods for higher education that have been mandated by some states, such as performance budgeting and funding, have began to address issues of cost containment in the form of examining program efficiency. However, some of the literature implies that there should be an improved understanding among state policy makers and institutions as to the performance indicators state colleges and universities are judged by and the quantifiable impact to cost containment efforts. Consequently, more research needs to be conducted to address the issues associated with this ongoing relationship between external governing bodies and state institutions of higher education.

Third, it should be noted that cost is discussed most often in terms of philosophical deliberations, the application of general principles, or in terms of

> **More research needs to be done to ascertain whether external bodies—such as government agencies—can best assess the cost efficiency of four-year colleges and universities.**

state or federal proposals and mandates. Thus, more is needed in terms of discussing the concrete terms of operation and the actual decision-making processes that are used to encourage cost containment. For example, it would be interesting to know if incentive-based containment efforts, selective cuts, or across-the-board cuts tend to be successful when employed at specific types of institutions or if one type of effort, in general, tends to produce the desired results at all types of institutions. Currently, as our research demonstrates, the cost incentives inherent in many institutions of higher education are not counteracted by incentives that lead to greater efficiency or cost containment. That is to say, "each institution type tends to spend up to the very limits of its means," (Bowen, 1980, p. 19) because to not do so could result in a reduced budget the following financial cycle.

Fourth, future research should address how to tailor concrete solution methods to specific academic settings and particular academic processes. What might work at a private institution may not work at a state institution or what might work at a large institution might not work at a small institution. To that end, a collection of case studies that addressed how a variety of distinct institutions have addressed a specific cost containment problem would make a valuable contribution to the work on containment efforts to date.

Fifth, it always needs to be understood that the economics of education constitute a dynamic enterprise that involves debating, developing, testing, and evaluating cost containment strategies and practices. It not only is the case that no one solution will work for all institutions, but it also is the case that one cannot be sure that a once-successful solution will continue to be an always-successful solution. Moreover, it is worth noting that some measures—"especially if pressed too far—are of dubious value, and some may already have been exploited to the limit" (Bowen, 1980, p. 22).

Sixth, we found that in engaging this dynamic enterprise and endeavor, each institution needs to determine how to secure the input of faculty, staff, and students in order to ensure that cost-saving measures will not be seen as capricious, and to ensure that cost efficiency is allied with the very practice of shared governance. To achieve shared governance, institutions of higher learning first must recognize when and where faculty and administrators are hindered from reaching consensus because of "restricted fields of vision." As Breslin explains,

> [p]residents and other senior staff members assume that the faculty has little comprehension of the world in which the administration needs to function in order to accomplish institutional goals. In many ways, the assumption is correct. Professors have become so specialized, so focused on their individual disciplines, that they no longer see the institution as a whole. I realize now, however, that administrators can have equally narrow perspective (Breslin, 2000, n.p.).

Therefore, to overcome these narrow perspectives and restricted fields of vision, administrators and faculty members must revisit their missions and refocus their strategies so that educational issues are preeminent and guide all decision making from assessing funding strategies to defining institutional goals.

Seventh, it should be understood that there are no simple solutions and there are no universal remedies. To that end, "administrators must weigh the advantages, disadvantages, and applicability of each strategy against the priorities, needs, and culture of the university to determine the best course of action" (Meyers, 1996, p. 69). Determining how to be cost efficient is a difficult task in and of itself; however, this task is further complicated by the fact that each institution not only must contain or cut costs, but also must do so while ensuring there is no loss to its reputation and distinctiveness. An institution's reputation and distinctiveness rests upon the quality of its faculty, and, as M. Peter McPherson, president of Michigan State University, argues, paradoxically, the very quality of its faculty may constitute one of the institution's major problems. As he points out, one of the problems with universities is that they "are filled with bright people with exceedingly good ideas, ideas that are difficult to prioritize in terms of where a given university's money should be spent" (qtd. in Brownstein, 2000). Therefore, in order not to compromise an institution's reputation and attractiveness, all cost containment decisions must be made with an eye to honoring and enhancing the institution's mission.

Eighth, as William Brand Simpson (1991) recommends, "[f]or involvement in budgeting to appear meaningful to the faculty, they must see it as providing an opportunity to influence outcomes that concern them, and they must be left with incentives to consider the possibility of doing things in a different way than they have done in the past" (p. 122). Moreover, because change is a constant, administrators and faculty members must plan for change through appropriate budgetary processes and through strategic planning. Strategic planning is vital to cost containment in that, at its best, it

- Promotes new initiatives rather than simply supporting existing areas that are performing well;
- Involves students and faculty as well as administrators;
- Provides incentives for change;
- Encourages goal setting that incorporates individual goals, departmental goals, and institutional goals in a comprehensive plan;
- Ensures that the achievement of the goals is measured;
- Couples diverse program units in the institution with the central bureaucracy;
- Prevents individuals from being reactive by calling upon them to anticipate problems and to recommend solutions; and
- Rewards responsiveness.

As Derek Bok, the president of Harvard University from 1971, noted: "If we are resourceful, there will be many ways for us to adapt and many unanticipated events that may change the picture. In the end, perhaps our greatest protection lies in our growing importance to the society that sustains us" (in Parnell, 1990). Each university and college is charged with deserving to be so sustained and so important, and one of the means of becoming deserving is to use society's resources responsibly and efficiently.

Ninth, we attempted to reveal through recounting the situations and stories of various private and public four-year institutions, some of the real issues and recommendations associated with cost containment efforts in a variety of expenditure areas such as plant operations and academic support. Although some of these cases were inconclusive, they provided additional insight as to how colleges and universities are struggling to rectify cost issues in their respective areas. In addition, where applicable, college and university cost issues were paralleled with cost issues associated with the corporate sector. For example, health care cost for employees in both sectors has varied as a result of changes in the method of health care delivery. It is recommend that institutions of higher education continue to gain further knowledge regarding the utilization of selected cost containment strategies from the private sector in an effort to maximize opportunities to fulfill their educational mission.

In the review of literature significant to explaining cost containment issues in four-year public and private institutions, this issue concentrates on material from a financial management perspective. Much of the past and current literature has been successful in addressing general economic theory in financing higher education (Bowen, 1980; Brinkman, 1990, 1992; Clotfelter, 1991; Winston, 1997; and Zemsky and Massy, 1990). In taking a different view, this issue presents a perspective specifically related to operating expenditures so that university administrators and academic program managers gain basic knowledge for practice and to aid the financial decision-making process. Where applicable, this issue draws comparisons to the private sector on cost issues and lessons learned. The vignettes further explain cost containment issues in higher education and provide ideas for application. This issue also concentrates on studies and analyses written primarily in the 1990s. The object was not to provide a comprehensive historical overview of cost containment efforts, but to organize critical issues and provoke thought on the subject during a period when the cost of operating both public and private institutions in higher education is of utmost concern (National Commission on the Cost of Higher Education, 1998).

Notes

[1]The work of Glassick and others makes a significant contribution to the area of faculty evaluation and reward as they relate to scholarship. Moreover, Glassick and others' work is commendable, in particular, because the writers address an array of faculty scholarship and discuss how such scholarship is recognized in a variety of university settings.

[2]In his analysis of the research university, Robert M. Rosenzweig (1998) confines himself to an examination of approximately 100 research institutions. As he explains in *The Political University: Policy, Politics, and Presidential Leadership in the American Research University,*

> [a]*lthough that may seem a small number—indeed, is a small number, in comparison with the total of 3,500 postsecondary institutions—it is a group whose influence and importance far exceed its percentage of the total. Not only do these universities conduct most of the nation's basic research; they also educate the vast majority of future college teachers and research scientists of all types as well as leaders of the learned professions. They are the most visible of all educational institutions, and, for better or worse, they are the models that many others in this country and abroad strive to emulate* (Rosenzweig, 1998, p. xiv).

Our analysis here encompasses a wider array of universities and practices and a greater number of cost containment practices; nonetheless, it is well worth recalling that it is indeed a small number of institutions that receive a major portion of federal funding for research and that also conduct a major portion of "the nation's basic research."

[3]According to Raiford (1998), dormitories have become a major marketing device for colleges and universities as students have become smart shoppers and colleges and universities have become savvy marketers. As a result, more and more universities are turning to architects, engineers, and interior designers who are able to design living quarters that are more homelike. Spacious individual accommodations with partial kitchens, carpet and

attractive wallcoverings, computer access, quality lighting control, and enhanced security are becoming more commonplace at both public and private colleges and universities (Raiford, 1998).

[4]While many colleges and universities include the administration of student aid under other administrative categories, for purposes of uniformity, we follow the guidelines of the Accounting Standards Booklet and include Student Aid under the Student Services category.

References

Abel-Kops, C. (2000, March). Wrestling with a Trojan horse: Outsourcing cataloging in academic and special libraries. *Catholic Library World, 70*(3), 175–177.

Abramson, P. (1997, January). Is deferred maintenance putting your college at risk? *College Planning & Management, 1*(1), 32–36.

Abramson, P. (1999, December). Is technology running the campus? *College Planning & Management, 12*(2), 16–17.

Abud, J. (1994). From contracted to in-house services at American universities. In *Contracting for facilities services.* Critical Issues in Facilities Management, no. 9. Alexandria, VA: Association of Higher Education Facilities Officers. (ED 408 872)

Accountability Task Force. *1993 Report of Governor's Task Force on University of Wisconsin Accountability Measures.* Madison, WI.

Adams, M. C. (1999, May/June). Public/private partnerships for new construction. *Facilities Manager, 15*(3), 9–10.

Ahumada, M. M. (1990). An analysis of state formula budgeting in higher education. In J. C. Smart (Ed.), *Higher education: Handbook of theory and research* (Vol. 6). New York: Agathon Press.

Allen, H. (1996). Faculty workload and productivity in the 1990s—preliminary findings. *NEA almanac of higher education.* Washington, DC: National Education Association.

American Association of State Colleges and Universities. (2000). *Special Report.* Washington, DC: American Association of State Colleges and Universities.

American Association of University Professors. (1986, January/February). 1940 statement of principles on academic freedom and tenure. *Academe, 72*(1), 52–54.

American Association of University Professors. (1998, March/April). Doing better. *Academe, 84,* 32.

American Council on Education. (1984). *1984-85 fact book on higher education.* New York: Macmillan.

American Institute of Certified Public Accountants. (1994). *Audits of colleges and universities.* New York: American Institute of Certified Public Accountants.

Anderson, R. E. (1988, June). The economy and higher education. *Capital Ideas, 3*(1).

Anonymous. (2001). California facilities devise strategies to deal with effects of energy crisis. *Facilities Design & Management, 20*(3), 9, 13.

Asher, B. T. (1994). *A president's perspective on student services delights and debits.* [On-line] Available: http://gateway.ovid.com (ED 366 855. 3 pp. MF-01; PC-01)

Ashworth, K. W. (1994, November/December). Performance-based funding in higher education: The Texas case study. *Change, 26*(6), 8–15.

Astin, A. W. (1993). *What matters in college: Four critical years revisited.* San Francisco: Jossey-Bass. (ED 351 927. 482 pp. MF-01; PC-01).

Astle, D., & Hamaker, C. (1986). Pricing by geography: British journal pricing 1986, including developments in other countries. *Library Acquisitions: Practice and Theory, 10,* 165–181.

Balderston, F. E. (1995). *Managing today's university.* San Francisco: Jossey-Bass.

Baldwin, R. G., & Chronister, J. L. (2001). *Teaching without tenure. Policies and practices for a new era.* Baltimore: Johns Hopkins University Press.

Banta, T. W., & Borden, V.M.H. (1994). *Performance indicators for accountability and improvement.* New Directions for Institutional Research, no. 82. San Francisco: Jossey-Bass.

Battin, P. (1982, September). Preservation: The forgotten problem (New Directions for Higher Education, no. 39). *Priorities for Academic Libraries, 10*(3), 61–70.

Baughman, J. C., & Goldman, R. N. (1997, November 24). The state of higher education. *The Boston Globe,* A13.

Benjamin, R., & Carrol, S. (1993). *Restructuring higher education—By design.* RAND (Issue Paper 2). Santa Monica, CA: Rand Distribution Services.

Benjamin, R., & Carrol, S. (1996). Impediments and imperatives in restructuring higher education. *Educational Administration Quarterly, 32,* 705–719.

Berdahl, R. O. (1974). *Problems in evaluating statewide boards.* In R. O. Berdahl (Ed.), *Evaluating statewide boards.* New Directions for Institutional Research, no. 5. San Francisco: Jossey-Bass.

Berne, R., & Schramm, R. (1986). *The financial analysis of governments.* Englewood Cliffs, NJ: Prentice-Hall.

Bessliata III, M. (1996). *Performance contracting for energy savings: A small college experience.* Proceeding of the 1996 Educational Conference and 83rd Annual Meeting, July 21–23, 1996. Salt Lake City, Utah.

Biddison G. B., & Hier, T. C. (1998). Build flexibility into ironclad agreements. *Trusteeship, 6*(1).

Bloland, P. A. (1992). Qualitative research in student affairs. *ERIC Digest.* Ann Arbor, MI: University of Michigan School of Education. (ED 347 487)

Blumenstyk, G. (2000, November 6). Ex-editor of journal says researchers should eschew financial ties to industry. *The Chronicle of Higher Education* [On-line]. Available: http://chronicle.com

Blumenstyk, G. (2001, February 9). Knowledge is a form of venture capital for a top Columbia administrator. *The Chronicle of Higher Education* [On-line]. Available: http://chronicle.com/search

Board of Regents Resolution. (1995, July 6). *The restructuring of the Montana University system phase two.* (ED 402 877)

Boatright, K. J. (1995). University of Wisconsin's system accountability. In G. H. Gaither (Ed.), *New directions for higher education, assessing performance in an age of accountability: Case studies* (pp. 51–64). San Francisco: Jossey-Bass.

Boer, William J. (1979, Spring). Long-range planning: An institutional priority. *Journal of the Indiana University Student Personnel Association* [On-line]. Available: http://gateway.ovid.com (ED 172 093. 9 pp. MF-01; PC-01)

Bogue, G. E. (1998). Quality assurance in higher education: The evolution of systems and design ideals. In *Quality assurance in higher education: An international perspective.* New Directions for Institutional Research, Vol. 25, no. 99. San Francisco: Jossey-Bass.

Bok, D. (1982). *Beyond the Ivory Tower: Social responsibility of the modern university.* Cambridge, MA: Harvard University Press.

Bok, D. (1990). Qtd. in D. Parnell.

Bok, D. (1992, July/August). Reclaiming the public trust *Change, 24*(4), 12–19.

Borden, V.M.H., & Bottrill, K. V. (1994, Summer). *Performance indicators: History, definitions, and methods.* New Directions for Institutional Research, no. 82. San Francisco: Jossey-Bass.

Boutwell, W. K. (1973). Formula budgeting on the down side. In G. Kaludis (Ed.), *Strategies for budgeting.* New Directions for Higher Education, no. 2. San Francisco: Jossey-Bass.

Bowen, H. R. (1980). *The cost of higher education: How much do colleges and universities spend per student and how much should they spend?* San Francisco: Jossey-Bass.

Bowen, H. R. (1983, January/February). The art of retrenchment. *Academe, 24*(1), 21–24.

Bowen, H. R., & Schuster, J. H. (1986). *American professor: A national resource imperiled.* New York: Oxford University Press.

Brainard, J., & Cordes, C. (1999, July 23). Pork-Barrel spending on academe reaches a record $797 million. *The Chronicle of Higher Education* [On-line]. Available: http://chronicle.com/search

Brainard, J., & Southwick, R. (2000, July 28). Congress gives colleges a billion-dollar bonanza: Embolden by budget surplus, lawmakers' earmark for specific institutions soar by 31%. *The Chronicle of Higher Education.*

Brainard, J., & Southwick, R. (2001, August 10). A record year at the federal trough: Colleges feast on $1.67 billion in earmarks budget surplus feeds congress's Pork-Barrel spending, intensifying criticism. *The Chronicle of Higher Education* [On-line]. Available: http://www.chronicle.com

Brawer, F. B. (1996, April). Retention-attrition in the nineties. *ERIC Digest.* Washington, DC: Educational Resources Information Center [On-line]. Available: http://gateway.ovid.com (ED 393 510. pp. 1–4. MF-01; PC-01)

Breneman, D. W. (1994). *On a collision course with new realities.* AGB Occassional Paper no. 22. Washington, DC: Association of Governing Boards of Universities and Colleges.

Breslin, R. D. (2000, November 10). Lessons from the presidential trenches. *The Chronicle of Higher Education* [On-line]. Available: http://chronicle.com/search

Brinkman, P. T. (1990). Higher education cost functions. In S. A. Hoenack & E. I. Collins (Eds.), *The economics of American universities.* Albany, NY: State University of New York Press.

Brinkman, P. T. (1992). Factors that influence cost in higher education. In C. S. Hollins (Ed.), *Containing cost and improving productivity in higher education.* New Directions for Institutional Research, no. 75. San Francisco: Jossey-Bass.

Brown, J. R., & Dev, C. S. (2000). Improving productivity in a service business: Evidence from the hotel industry. *Journal of Service Research, 2*(4), 339–354.

Brown, S., & Hunsicker, S. L. (1999). *Electric restructuring and utilities deregulation: A facility manager's guide.* Alexandria, VA: The Association of Higher Education Facilities Officers.

Brown, S. L. (1998). Statewide policy issues—Being a player. *Electric restructuring and utilities deregulation: A facility manager's guide.* Alexandria, VA: The Association of Higher Education Facilities Officers.

Brownstein, A. (2000, October 17). Tuition climbs at public and private colleges. College board reports. *The Chronicle of Higher Education, 47* [On-line]. Available: http://chronicle.com

Brownstein, A. (2000, October 27). Tuition rises faster than inflation, and faster than in previous year. *The Chronicle of Higher Education, 47,* A50.

Bruce, S., & Hunt, C. (1996). Publishing, economics, and the academy: Faculty perspective on the bottom line. *The Bottom Line: Managing Library Finances, 9*(2), 6–9.

Bucklin, L. P. (1977). Structures, conduct and productivity in distribution. In H. B. Thorelli (Ed.), *Strategy + Structure = Performance* (pp. 219–236). Bloomington, IN: Indiana University Press.

Bureau of Labor Statistics. (1999). *Employee benefits survey* [On-line]. Available: http://www.bls.gov/ news.release/ebs.3.t05.htm

Burgan, M. (1996, November 25). Should colleges and universities abolish academic tenure? *News World Communications, Inc.*

Burke, J. (1998). *Managing campus budgets in trying times: Did practices follow principles?* Albany, NY: The Nelson A. Rockefeller Institute of Government.

Burke, J. C., & Serban, A. M. (1998). State synopsis of performance funding programs. In J. C. Burke & A. M. Serban (Eds.), *Performance funding in public higher education: Fad or trend?* New Directions for Institutional Research, Vol. 25, no. 97. San Francisco: Jossey-Bass.

Burke, J. C., Modarresi, S., & Serban, A. M. (1999). Performance: Shouldn't it count for something in state budgeting? *Change, 31*(6), 16–21.

Cage, M. C. (1995, June 2). New Florida University to offer an alternative to tenure. *The Chronicle of Higher Education, 41* [On-line]. Available: http://chronicle.com

Callan, P., & Finney, J. E. (Eds.). (1997). *Public and private financing of higher education: Shaping public policy for the future.* Phoenix, AZ: American Council on Education and the Oryx Press.

Carlson, T. R. (2000). Benefit cost management in the new millennium. *Benefits Quarterly, 16*(2), 28–32.

Carnevale, D. (1999, September 10). Legislatures and public colleges wrangle over tuition and fees. *The Chronicle of Higher Education, 46* [On-line]. Available: http://chronicle.com

Carnevale, D. (2000, April 28). Student services will be online across the south. *The Chronicle of Higher Education, 46* [On-line]. Available: http://chronicle.com

Carter, K. (1994). *The performance budget revisited* (Legislative Finance Paper #91). Denver, CO: National Conferences of State Legislatures.

Casper, G. (1995, April 18). *Come the Millennium, Where the University?* Keynote address, American Educational Research Association Annual Meeting. San Francisco, CA.

Cave, M., Hanney, S., Henkel, M., & Kogan, M. (1997). *The use of performance indicators in higher education.* London: Bristol, PA: J. Kingsley.

Chait, R. (1997, February 7). Why academe needs more employment options. *The Chronicle of Higher Education, 43,* B4.

Chait, R., & Ford, A. T. (1982). *Beyond traditional tenure.* San Francisco: Jossey-Bass.

Cho, M., & Bero, L. A. (1996). The quality of drug studies published in symposium proceedings. *Annals of Internal Medicine, 124,* 485–489.

Chronicle of Higher Education. (2001, August 31). *Almanac Issue.* Washington, DC: National Education Association.

Chronicle of Higher Education. (1998, August 28). *Almanac Issue.* Washington, DC: National Education Association.

Chronister, J. L. (1996). Benefits and retirement: A changing environment. *The NEA 1996 almanac of higher education* (pp. 99–109). Washington, DC: National Education Association.

Chronister, J. L. (2000). Benefits and retirement: Challenges for the new century. *The NEA almanac of higher education* (pp. 73–90). Washington, DC: National Education Association.

Chronister, J. L., & Kepple, T. R., Jr. (1987). *Incentive early retirement programs for faculty: Innovative responses to a changing environment.* Washington, DC: Association for the Study of Higher Education; ERIC Clearinghouse on Higher Education. (ED 283 478)

Clark, M. C. (1976). *Class size and college teaching: Attitudes and preferences.* Washington, DC: ERIC Clearinghouse on Higher Education. (ED 126 834)

Clery S. B., & Lee, J. B. (2000). Faculty salaries, 1998-99. *The NEA almanac of higher education.* Washington, DC: National Education Association.

Clotfelter, C. T. (1991). *Economic challenges in higher education.* Chicago: University of Chicago Press.

Clotfelter, C. T. (1996). Buying the best: Cost escalation in elite higher education. Princeton, NJ: Princeton University Press.

Cohen, C. M. (1998). *The shaping of American higher education: Emergence and growth of the contemporary system.* San Francisco: Jossey-Bass.

Coll, M., & Von Seggern, D. J. (1991, May). *Community college student retention: Some procedural and programmatic suggestions.* Paper presented at the Wyoming Higher Education Student Affairs Conference, 22–24 May, 1991. Powell, Wyoming. (ED 345 816. 10 pp. MF-01; PC-01)

College and University Personnel Association. (1997). *1998-99 National faculty survey by discipline and rank in public colleges and universities.* Washington, DC.

Compensation Commission. (1992). *Report of the governor's commission on University of Wisconsin system compensation.* Madison, WI.

Coombs, P. H., & Hallak, J. (1987). *Cost analysis in education: A tool for policy and planning.* Baltimore: The Johns Hopkins University Press.

Cordes, C. (1996, May 17). Government issues new rules on reimbursing research overhead. *The Chronicle of Higher Education, 42,* A32.

Council for Aid to Education. (1997). *Breaking the social contract. The fiscal crisis in higher education.* Council for Aid to Education. Subsidiary of RAND.

Council on Library and Information Resources. (1999, August). *Innovative use of information technology by colleges.* Washington, DC: Council on Library and Information Resources.

Davies, E. (1998). Strategic issues in managing information and document supply in academic libraries. *Library Management, 19*(5), 318–326.

DeHayes, D. W., & Lovrinic, J. G. (1994). *Activity based costing model for assessing economic performance.* New Directions for Institutional Research, no. 82. San Francisco: Jossey-Bass.

Delano, D. (2000). Employer cost moved marginally higher during 1999. *Electronic Business, 26*(4), 19–20.

Derlin, R. (1996). *An academic department's response to outcomes assessment.* Paper presented at the New Mexico Higher Education Assessment Conference, February 22–23, 1996. Albuquerque, New Mexico. (ED 400 760. pp. 1–20, MF-01; PC-01)

Diamond, R. M. (1994). *Serving on promotion and tenure committees.* Bolton, MA: Anker Publishing.

Dickmeyer, N. (1992). Budgeting. In D. W. Breneman, L. Leslie, & R. E. Anderson (Eds.), *ASHE reader on finance in higher education,* Needham Heights, MA: Simon & Schuster Custom Publishing.

Dill, D., & Sporn, B. (Eds.). (1995). Emerging patterns of social demand and university reform. Through a glass darkly. *Issues in Higher Education.* Conference Proceedings, Paris, France: International Association of University of Paris.

Dochy, F.J.R.C., Segers, M.S.R., & Wijnen, W.H.F.W. (Eds.). (1990). *Management information and performance indicators in higher education: An international issue.* The Netherlands: Van Gorcum.

Doctrow, J., Sturtz, C., & Lawrence, S. (1996). Private university properties. *Planning for Higher Education, 24,* 18–22.

Dolence, M. G., & Norris D. M. (1994). *Using key performance indicators to drive strategic decision making.* New Directions for Institutional Research, no. 82. San Francisco: Jossey-Bass.

Duchin, D. (1998). Outsourcing Newman library, Baruch College/CUNY. *The Bottom Line: Managing Library Finances, 11*(3), 111–115.

Duffey, J. D. (1992, Fall). What's ahead for higher education? The future isn't what it used to be. *Education Record, 73*(4), 6–10. (EJ 453 167)

Dwyer, J. (1999). Consortia review and purchase networked resources: The California State University experience. *The Bottom Line: Managing Library Finances, 1*, 5–11.

Eaton, J. S. (1995). *Investing in American higher education: An argument for restructuring.* New York: Council for Aid to Education.

Ehrenberg, R. G. (1997). The case for tenure; book reviews. *Industrial and Labor Relations Review, 51*(1), 138.

Ehrenberg, R. G. (2000). *Tuition rising: Why colleges cost so much.* Cambridge, MA: Harvard University Press.

El-Khawas, E. (1994). Restructuring initiatives in public higher education: Institutional response to financial constraints. *Research Briefs, 5*(8).

El-Khawas, E. (1995). Campus trends 1995. New directions for academic programs. Higher education panel (Report no. 85). Washington, DC: American Council on Education.

Employee Benefits Research Institute. (1998, September 1). *EBRI News* [On-line]. Available: http://www.ebri.org

Ender, E. L., & Mooney, K. A. (1994, Winter). From outsourcing to alliances: Strategies for sharing leadership and exploiting resources at metropolitan universities. *Metropolitan Universities: An International Forum, 5*(3), 51–60. (EJ 499 519)

Eng, L., & Heller, K. Faculty are spending less time teaching.

English, R., & Hardesty, L. (2000, June). Create change: Shaping the future of scholarly journal publishing. *C & RL News.*

Epstein, G. (1999). Economic beat: There's a minor upside to corporate downsizing. *Barron's, 79*(45), 52–53.

Ewell, P. T. (1988). Outcome, assessment and academic improvement: In search of useable knowledge. In *Higher education: Handbook of theory and research.* New York: Agathon Press.

Executive Order No. 177, 1993.

Fairweather, J. (1993, July/August). Faculty rewards reconsidered: The nature of tradeoffs. *Change, 25*(4).

Fickes, M. (1999). To renovate or build? *College Planning & Management, 5*, 22–24.

Figg, J. (2000, June). Outsourcing: A runaway train. *The Internal Auditor, 57*(3), 48.

Filippello, A. N. (1999, January). The evolution of restructuring: Seizing change to create value. *Business Economics, 34*(1), 25–28.

Fisher, J. (1997). *Comparing electronic journals to print journals: Are there savings?* Paper presented at the Conference on Scholarly Communications and Technology, April 24–25, 1997. Atlanta, Georgia [On-line]. Available: http://www.arl/scomm/scat/ (ED 414 917)

Flanagan, J. S. (1991). *Planning for healthy university facilities.* Alexandria, VA: Association of Higher Education Facilities Officers.

Florida State Postsecondary Commission. (1995, December). *Postsecondary accountability review: Report and recommendation of the Florida Postsecondary Education Planning Commission.* (ED 393 382)

Folger, J. (Ed.). (1984). *Financial incentives for academic quality.* San Francisco: Jossey-Bass.

Fox-Penner, P., & Basheda, G. (2001, Spring). A short honeymoon for utility deregulation. *Issues in Science and Technology,* 17, 51–56.

Frank, R. H. (1999). *Higher education: The ultimate winner take all market.* Paper presented at the Forum for the Future of Higher Education, September 27, 1999. Aspen, Colorado.

Freeman, L. (1996). Comprehensive conservation: The center for energy and environmental education was built with the environment in mind. *School Planning & Management,* c1–c3.

Freeman, T. (1994). *State university of New York. Performance indicators report.* State University of New York, Albany. (ED 403 865. 3 pp. MF-01; PC-02.)

Freeman, T. F. (1995). *Performance indicators and assessment in the State University of New York system.* New Directions for Higher Education, no. 91. San Francisco: Jossey-Bass.

Frost, S. H. (1991). *Academic advising for student success: A system of shared responsibility.* ASHE-ERIC Higher Education Report, no. 3. Washington, DC: The George Washington University. (ED 339 272. 118 pp. MF-01; PC-05)

Gappa, J. M. (1984). Employing part-time faculty: Thoughtful approaches to continuing problems. *AAHE Bulletin, 37*(2), 3–7.

Gappa, J. M., & Leslie, D. W. (1997, January 1). Two faculties or one? The conundrum of part-time in a bifurcation work force. *New pathways: Faculty career and employment for the 21st century working paper series, inquiry #6.* American Association for the Advancement of Science, 1–33. (ED 424 817)

Gardner, D. (1983). *A nation at risk: The imperative for educational reform. An open letter to the American people.* A Report to the Nation and the Secretary of Education. (ED 226 006)

Gardner, M. (1994). Contracted custodial services at Butler University. In *Contracting for facilities services.* Critical Issues in Facilities Management, no. 9. Alexandria, VA: The Association of Higher Education Facilities Officers. (ED 408 872)

Garland, P. H., & Grace, T. W. (1993). *New perspectives for student affairs professionals: Evolving realities, responsibilities, and roles.* ASHE-ERIC Higher Education Report, no. 7. Washington, DC: The George Washington University, School of Education and Human Development. (ED 370 508. 152 pp. MF-01; PC-07)

Gaylord, T. A., & Rogers, B. (1988). *Restructuring the university of Alaska statewide system of higher education.* Paper presented at the Annual International Conference of the Society for College and University Planning 23rd, July 31–Aug 3, 1988. Toronto Ontario, Canada. (ED 311 794. 18 pp.)

Getz, M. (1997). *Electronic publishing in academia: An economic perspective.* Paper presented at the Conference on Scholarly Communications and Technology, April 24–25, 1997. Atlanta, Georgia. (ED 414 918. 31 pp. MF-01; PC-02)

Getz, M., Gullette, J. M., Kilpatrick, D. E., & Siegfried, J. J. (1994). The make or buy decision: The organization of U.S. campus plant operations. In *Contracting for facilities services.* Critical Issues in Facilities Management, no. 9. Alexandria, VA: The Association of Higher Education Facilities Officers. (ED 408 872)

Giffin, R. E. (1990). Selecting a guaranteed energy savings contract. In *Critical issues in facilities management.* Alexandria, VA: Association of Physical Plant Administrators of Universities and Colleges.

Givens, L. (1995, June). Budget philosophy 101. Encouraging utility efficiency. *NACUBO Business Officer, 28*(12), 34–36.

Glassick, C. E., Huber, M. T., & Maeroff, G. I. (1997). *Scholarship assessed: Evaluation of the professoriate.* San Francisco: Jossey-Bass.

Glenny, L. A., & Schmidtlein, F. A. (1980). *The role of the state in the governance of higher education.* Program Report, no. 80-B16. Stanford University, CA: Institute for Research on Educational Finance and Governance. (ED 194 996)

Gobstein, H. (1986). Who's going to pay to maintain research excellence at U.S. universities? In M. McKeown & K. Alexander (Eds.), *Values in conflict: Funding priorities for higher education* (pp. 239–259). Cambridge, MA: Ballinger.

Goldstien, P. J., Kempner, D. E., & Rush, S. C. (1993). *Contact management or self-operation: A decision-making guide for higher education.* Alexandria, VA: Association of Higher Education Facilities Officers. (ED 375 704)

Goldstien, P. J., Kempner, D. E., & Rush, S. C. (1994). Making the contract or self-operation decision. In *Contracting for facilities services.* Critical Issues in Facilities Management, no. 9. Alexandria, VA: Association of Higher Education Facilities Officers. (ED 408 872)

Goodman, D. (2000, June 15). The new consortia: "Where's the fiscal sense?" *Library Journal.*

Gose, B. (1998, March). Tutoring companies take over remedial education at some colleges. Can Kaplan and Sylvan help students erase educational deficiencies more quickly? In T. Kaganoff (Ed.), *Collaboration, technology, and outsourcing initiatives in higher education: A literature review.* Paper prepared by RAND for the Foundation for Independent Higher Education.

Goudy, F. (1993). Academic libraries and the six percent solution: A twenty-year financial overview. *Journal of Academic Librarianship, 19*(4), 212–215.

Governor's Commission. (1993, December 31). *Report of the governor's higher education review commission* (Vol. 1, Report; Vol. II, Appendices). Frankfort, KY: Kentucky Council on Higher Education.

Green, K. C. (1997). *1996 campus computing survey.* (ED 405 762. 38 pp. MF-01; PC not available) EDRS [On-line]. Available: http://ericr.svr.edu/Projects/Campus computing

Green, K. C., & Gilbert, S. W. (1995, March/April). Great expectations: Content, communications, productivity and the role of information technology in higher education. *Change, 27*(2), 8–18.

Green, K. C., & Gilbert, S. W. (1995, January/February). Academic productivity and technology. *Academe, 81,* 19–25.

Griffin, J. (1998, March/April). Third-party project management: A coming reality for an increasingly unrealistic world. *Facilities Manager, 14*(2), 19–23. (EJ 564 070)

Grimm, J. C. (1986, Winter). New ideas in facility management. *Journal of College & University Student Housing, 16*(2), 3–5.

Guthrie, K. (1997, January 1). JSTOR: The development of a cost-driven, value-based pricing model. In *Technology and scholarly communication.* The Andrew W. Mellon Foundation.

Hackett, R. E., & Morgan, T. (1996). The deferred maintenance crisis: A comparison of smaller state-supported and independent institutions. *Educational Facility Planner, 33*(3), 18–23.

Hammer, M., & Champy, J. (1993). *Reengineering the corporation: A manifesto for business revolution.* New York: HarperCollins.

Handy, C. (1994). *The age of paradox.* Cambridge, MA: Harvard Business School Press.

Hatzia, G. (1998, June). Conservation is job one. *Business Officer, 3*(12), 22–24.

Hauptman, A. M. (2001). Reforming the ways states finance higher education. In D. E. Heller (Ed.), *The state and public higher education policy. Affordability, access and accountability* (pp. 64–80). Baltimore: The Johns Hopkins University Press.

Hawkins, B. (1996). Planning for the national electronic library. *Educom Review, 31*(3) [Online]. Available: http://www.educause.edu/pub/er/review/reviewArticles/29319.html

Hawkins, B. (1999). A dozen thoughts to stir the pot. In *Innovative use of information technology by colleges* (pp. 17–19). Washington, DC: Council on Library and Information Resources.

Haworth, K. (1997, October 24). Penn may lay off 175 after hiring company to manage properties. *The Chronicle of Higher Education.*

Hearn, J. C. (1999). Pay and performance in the university: An examination of faculty salaries. *The Review of Higher Education, 22*(4), 391–410.

Heller, D. (1999). The effects of tuition and state financial aid on public college enrollment. *The Review of Higher Education, 23*(1), 65–89.

Hill, J. S. (1998). Boo! Outsourcing from the cataloging perspective. *Bottom Line: Managing Library Finances, 11*(3), 116–121.

Hines, E. R. (1988). *Higher education and state governments: Renewed partnership, cooperation, or competition.* ASHE-ERIC/Higher Education Research Report, no. 5. Washington, DC: The George Washington University/ERIC.

Hines, E. R., & Highman, J., III. (1996, November). *Faculty work load and state policy.* Paper presented at a meeting of the Association for the study of Higher Education, Memphis, Tennessee.

Hitt, M. A, Ireland, R. D., & Hoskisson, R. E. (1995). *Strategic management: Competitiveness and globalization* (pp. 942–960). St. Paul, MN: West.

Hopkins, D. (1990). The higher education production function: Theoretical foundations and empirical findings. In S. Hoenack & E. Collins (Eds.), *The economics of American universites* (pp. 11–32). Albany, NY: SUNY Press.

Howard-Hamilton, M. F., Phelps, R. E., & Torres, V. (1998, Summer). Meeting the needs of all students and staff members: The challenge of diversity. *New Directions for Student Services, 82*, 49–64. (EJ 576 979)

Hoxby, C. (2000). The return to attending a highly selective college. *Futures forum 2000.* (pp. 14–17). Cambridge, MA: Forum for the Future of Higher Education 2000.

Huber, R. M. (1992). *How professors play the cat guarding the cream: Why we are paying more and getting less in higher education.* Fairfax, VA: George Mason University Press.

Hughes, C. A., Rockman, I., & Wilson, L. A. (2000). Communicating resource needs for successful library services. *Bottom Line: Managing Library Finances, 13*(1), 10–15.

Huish, J., & van der Have, P. J. (1998, March/April). The value in value management: A dialogue. *Facilities Manager, 14*(2), 31, 33, 36–37, 39, 41.

Hunsicker, S. R. (1998). Legal/regulatory background and status report. In *Electric restructuring and utilities deregulation: A facility manager's guide.* Alexandria, VA: The Association of Higher Education Facilities Managers.

Hyatt, J. A., Shulman, C. H., & Santiago, M. (1984). *Strategies for effective resources management.* Washington, DC: National Association of College and University Business Officers.

Illinois State Board of Higher Education. (1997, January 7). *Fiscal year 1998 higher education budget recommendations: Operations and grants.* Springfield, IL: Illinois Board of Higher Education. (ED 408 857)

Illinois State Board of Higher Education. (1995, May 2). *Update on expenditure trends in Illinois higher education* (Item No. 5c). Springfield, IL: Illinois Board of Higher Education. (ED 382 067)

Illinois State Board of Higher Education. (1997, January). *Fiscal year 1998 higher education budget recommendation: Operation and grants.* Springfield, IL: Illinois Board of Education. (ED 403 857)

Jacobson, P. D. (1999, July/August). Challenges to managed care cost containment programs: An initial assessment. *Health Affairs.* [On-line]. Available: http://www.proquest.umi.com

Jacoby, S. M. (1999). Are career jobs headed for extinction? *California Management Review, 42*(1), 123–145.

Johannesen, R. (1999). Satisfaction = Revenue. *Business Officer, 32*(10), 42–45. (EJ 584 125)

Johnson, K. (1996). *Forging a new partnership between schools and electric utilities.* Proceeding of the 1996 Educational Conference and 83rd Annual Meeting, July 21–23, 1996. Salt Lake City, Utah.

Johnstone, D. B. (1998, Spring). Patterns of finance: Revolution, evolution, or more of the same? *Review of Higher Education, 21*(3), 245–255. (EJ 562 846)

Joint Commission on Accountability Reporting. (1995). *A need answered: An executive summary of recommended accountability formats.* Washington, DC: American Association of State Colleges and Universities.

Jones, D. (1984). *Higher education budgeting at the state level: Concepts and principles.* Boulder, CO: NCHEMS.

Jones, D. (1997). Perspectives on performance funding: Concepts, practices, and principles. (Unpublished draft.)

Joyce, P., & Mertz, T. (1985). Price discrimination in academic journals. *Library Quarterly, 55,* 273–283.

Julio, B. (1997). Power pedagogy: Integrating technology in the classroom. *Proceedings of the Association of Small Computer Users in Education,* 112–125. (ED 410 927)

Kaganoff, T. (1998). *Collaboration, Technology, and Outsourcing Initiatives in Higher Education: A Literature Review.* RAND/MR-973-EDU, Santa Monica, CA: RAND.

Kaiser, H. H. (1993). *The facilities audit. A process for improving facilities conditions.* Alexandria, VA: Association of Higher Education Facilities Officers. (ED 408 875)

Kaiser, H. H., & Davis, J. S. (1996). *A foundation to uphold: A study of facilities conditions at U.S. colleges and universities.* Alexandria, VA: The Association of Higher Education Facilities Officers. (ED 406 919)

Kane, T. J. (1997). Beyond tax relief: Long-term challenges in financing higher education. *National Tax Journal, 50*(2), 335–349.

Kantor, P. B. (1985). The relationship between cost and services at academic libraries. In P. Spyers-Duran & T. W. Mann (Eds.), *Financing information services: Problems, changing approaches, and new opportunities for academic and research libraries.* Westport, CT: Greenwood.

Kaplin, W. A., & Lee, B. A. (1997). *A legal guide for students affairs professionals.* San Francisco: Jossey-Bass.

Karkia, M. R. (1997). Energy management and conservation. In *Part III: Energy and utilities systems.* Alexandria, VA: The Association for Higher Education Facilities Officers.

Karr, S., & Kelley, R. V. (1996, Summer). *Attracting new sources of research funding.* New Directions for Higher Education, no. 94 . San Francisco: Jossey-Bass.

Kells, H. R. (1990). The inadequacy of performance indicators for higher education: The need for a more comprehensive and development construct. *Higher Education Management, 2*(3), 258–270.

Kennedy, D. (1995, May/June). Another century's end, another revolution for higher education. *Change, 27,* 8–15.

Kentucky Council of Higher Education. Council Meetings, Agenda Attachments, May 1, 1994; November 13, 1995; March 4, May 20, 1996.

Kentucky General Assembly. Regular Session 1996: Senate Concurrent Resolution No. 93. Creating a Task Force on Postsecondary Education. March 5, 1996.

Kerr, C. (1991, May/June). The new race to be Harvard or Berkeley or Stanford. *Change, 23*(3), 8–15.

King, R. T., Jr. (1996, April 25). How a drug firm paid for a university study, then undermined it. *Wall Street Journal,* pp. A1 13.

Larger, C., & Klinger, D. (1998, November). Enhancing economic and institutional strength. *Business Officer, 32*(5), 33–37.

Layzell, D. T. (1996). Faculty workload and productivity: Recurrent issues with new imperatives. *Review of Higher Education,19*(3), 267–281.

Layzell, D. T. (1996). Developments in state funding for higher education. *Higher education: Handbook of theory and research* (Vol. 4). New York: Agathon Press.

Layzell, D. T. (1998). Linking performance to funding outcomes for public institutions of higher education: The U.S. experience. *European Journal of Education, 33*(1), 103–111.

Leatherman, C. (1999, April 9). Growth in positions off the tenure track is a trend that's here to stay, study finds. *The Chronicle of Higher Education, 45*(3) [On-line]. Available: http://chronicle.com

Lenth, C. S. (1993, December). *The tuition dilemma: State policies and practices in pricing public higher education.* Denver, CO: State Higher Education Executive Officers.

Leslie, L. L., & Rhoades, G. (1995, March/April). Rising administrative costs: Seeking explanations. *Journal of Higher Education, 66*(2), 187–212. (EJ 499 697)

Libby, K. A., & Caudle, D. M. (1997, November). A survey on the outsourcing of cataloging in academic libraries. *College and Research Libraries, 58*(6), 550–560.

Lipman-Blumen, J. (1998). Connective leadership: What business needs to learn from academe. *Change, 30*(1), 49.

Louisiana Board of Regents. Press Release. Aug. 26, 1997.

Lyddon, J. W., Fonte, R., & Miller, J. L. (1986, March). *Toward a framework to analyze state funding in higher education.* Paper presented at the 1986 Annual Meeting of the Association for the Study of Higher Education, San Diego, California.

MacTaggart, T. (1996). *Restructuring higher education.* San Francisco: Jossey-Bass.

Magner, D. (1995, March 31). Tenure re-examined. *The Chronicle of Higher Education, 41*, A17.

Magner, D. (1998, October 23). Tenure will be harder to get, experts say, but it won't disappear. *The Chronicle of Higher Education, 45* [On-line]. Available: http://chronicle.com

Majka, D. (2000). The great exchange: The economic promise and peril of the digital library. *The Bottom Line: Managing Library Finances, 13*(2), 68–73.

Martin, M. S. (1998). Library management of electronic information: Reports on recent conferences. *The Bottom Line: Managing Library Finances, 11*(1), 24–27.

Maryland Higher Education Commission, Maryland (1998). *Performance accountability report. Maryland public colleges and universities.* Annapolis, MD: Maryland Higher Education Commission. (ED 425 681)

Massy, W. F. (1987). Making it all work: Sound financial management. *New Directions for Higher Education, 58*, 87–102.

Massy, W. F. (1996). *Resource allocation in higher education.* Ann Arbor, MI: University of Michigan Press.

Massy, W. F. (1996, Winter). New thinking on academic restructuring. *AGB Priorities,* 1–16.

Massy, W., & Wilger, A. K. (1995). Improving productivity: What faculty think about it and its effects on quality. *Change, 27*(4), 10–20.

Massy, W. F., & Zemskey, R. (1990, March 2). *The dynamics of academic productivity: A seminar.* Denver, CO: State Higher Education Executive Officers Association. (ED 327 079)

Massy, W. F. (1991, September/October). Improving academic productivity: The new frontier? *Capital Ideas, 6,* 1–14.

Massy, W. F. (1995). *Using information technology to enhance academic productivity.* Washington, DC: EDUCOM.

Matasek, D. (1999, June). The balance of power. *American School & University, 71*(10), 30, 32, & 34.

Matteson, G. (1995). Electrical energy services options: Deregulation presents new opportunities. *Business Officer, 28*(12), 37–43.

Matthews, G. J., & Curry, J. A. (1995, May/June). Back to the drawing board. *Trusteeship,* 13–17.

McGuinness, A. C., Jr. (1995). *Restructuring state roles in higher education. A case study of the 1994 New Jersey Higher Education Restructuring Act.* Denver, CO: Education Commission of the States. (ED 394 457)

McGuinness, A. C., Jr., & Ewell, P. T. (1994, Fall). Improving productivity and quality in higher education. *AGB Priorities, 2,* 1–12.

McKeown-Moak, M. (1999). *Financing higher education: An annual report from the states.* Denver, CO: State Higher Education Executive Officers. (ED 428 638)

McIntyre, J. (1995, June). Power play: Energy reduction programs help campuses tighten belts. *Business Officer, 28*(12), 30–33.

McPherson, M., & Schapiro, M. O. (1998). *The student aid game: Meeting need and rewarding talent in American higher education.* Princeton, NJ: Princeton University Press.

Meisinger, R. J. (1994). College and university budgeting: An introduction for faculty and academic administrators. National Association of College and University Business Officers, One Duport Circle, Washington, DC. (ED 378 911)

Meyer, K. A. (1998). *Faculty workload studies: Perspectives, needs, and future directions.* ASHE-ERIC Higher Education Report, no. 1. Washington, DC: The George Washington University, Graduate School of Education and Human Development. (ED 416 655)

Meyers, R. S. (1996, Summer). *Restructuring to sustain excellence.* New Directions for Higher Education, no. 94. San Francisco: Jossey-Bass.

Michaelson, M. (1998). Automate your physical plant using the building block approach. *College Planning & Management, 1*(4), 37–42.

Middaugh, M. F. (2001). *Understanding faculty productivity, standards and benchmarks for colleges and universities.* San Francisco: Jossey-Bass.

Montana University System Board of Regents (1995, July 6). *The restructuring of the Montana University system: Phase two board of regents resolution.* Helena, MT: Montana University System. (ED 402 877)

Morgan, A. W. (1983, May/June). Cost as a policy issue: Lessons from the health-care sector. *Journal of Higher Education, 54*(3), 279–293. (EJ 281 274)

Nanus, B. (1992). Visionary leadership: Creating a new tomorrow. In *Perspective on leadership in facilities management.* Alexandria, VA: The Association of Higher Education Facilities Officers.

Nauman, M. (1997). Vendors and academic libraries: Development and change. *The Bottom Line: Managing Library Finances, 10*(4), 165–168.

National Academy of Sciences. (1989). *Government-university-industry research roundtable. Science and technology in the academic enterprise: Status, trends, and issues.* Washington, DC: National Academy of Sciences.

National Center for Educational Statistics. (1999). *Integrated postsecondary education data system, restricted salary data, 1998-99.* Washington, DC: National Center for Educational Statistics.

National Commission on the Cost of Higher Education. (1998). *Straight talk about college costs and prices.* Phoenix, AZ: The Oryx Press.

National Education Association. (2000). *Almanac of higher education.* Washington, DC: National Education Association.

Naylor, H. T., & William, H. (1997). *Downsizing the USA.* Grand Rapids, MI: Wm. B. Eerdmans Publishing.

Neal, J. (1997). *The use of electronic scholarly journals: Models of analysis and data drawn from the project MUSE experience at Johns Hopkins University.* Paper presented at the Conference on Scholarly Communication and Technology, April 24–25, 1997. Atlanta, Georgia [On-line]. Available: http://www.arl.org/scomm/scat

Neal, J. E. (1995). *Overview of policy and practice: Differences and similarities in developing higher education. Accountability.* New Directions for Higher Education, no. 91. San Francisco: Jossey-Bass.

Nedwek, B. (1996). Public policy and public trust: The use and misuse of performance indicators in higher education. In John C. Smart (Ed.), *Higher education handbook of theory and research.* Bronx, NY: Agathon Press.

Nelson, C. (1999, April 16). The war against the faculty. *The Chronicle of Higher Education, 45* [On-line]. Available: http://chronicle.com.

Nettles, M. T. (1995). The National Policy Agenda on higher education assessment: A wake-up call. *The Review of Higher Education, 18*(3), 293–313.

Nettles, M. T., & Cole, J. (2001). A study in tension: State assessment and public colleges and universities. In D. E. Heller (Ed.), *The states and public higher education policy, affordability, access and accountability.* Baltimore: The Johns Hopkins University Press.

New Jersey Commission on Higher Education. (1999). *The five-year assessment of higher education restructuring.* A joint report of the New Jersey Commission on higher education and the New Jersey president's council. (ED 432 355)

New Mexico Commission on Higher Education. (1997). *Higher education funding recommendations 1998-99.* Santa Fe, NM: New Mexico Commission on Higher Education. New York State Office of Comptroller. (ED 420 271)

Nicklin, J. L. (1996, April 5). Five colleges in Boston to combine some operations to cut costs. *The Chronicle of Higher Education, 42,* A34.

Novak, R. J. (1996). Methods, objectives, and consequences of restructuring. In T. J. MacTaggart (Ed.), *Restructuring higher education* (pp. 16–49). San Francisco: Jossey-Bass.

Nuzzo, D. (1999, May). Don't outsource it. Do it. *Library Journal, 124*(8), 46–48.

Nyquist, E. B. (1970). *Some comments on the financial problems of private colleges.* Speech made on December 7, 1970, at the panel discussion held at Marymount College.

O'Donnell, J. P., & Newman, I. (2000). The changing role of the chief information officer in higher education. In D. E. Williams & E. D. Garten (Eds.), *Advances in library administration and organization.* Philadelphia: JAI Press.

Okerson, A. (1986, November). Periodical prices: A history and discussion. *Advances in Serials Management, 1,* 101–134.

O'Leary, C. (2000, December 11). California turmoil shakes, but can't stop. The boom in utility finance: High costs, tottering power companies and legal questions abound. *The Investment Dealer's Digest,* 16–17.

Olsen, F. (2001, January 29). Princeton will eliminate loans for undergraduates and make graduate stipends more generous. *The Chronicle of Higher Education* [On-line]. Available: http://chronicle.com/search

O'Neill, J. M. (1998, June 13). Downsizing measures invade nation's campuses. *The Philadelphia Inquirer.*

Oregon State Board of Higher Education. (1995, April). *Higher education assessment and accountability.* Eugene, OR: Oregon State System of Higher Education. (ED 394 476)

Osif, B. A., & Harwood, R. L. (2000). Privatization and outsourcing. *Library Administration & Management, 14*(2), 102–107.

Parnell, D. (1990). *Dateline 2000: The new higher education agenda.* Washington, DC: Community College Press.

Pastine, M. (1996). Academic libraries and campus computing costs. *The Bottom Line: Managing Library Finances, 9*(3), 20–32.

Patton, P. E. (1997, March 26). An agenda for the 21st century: A plan for post-secondary education in Kentucky. Frankfort, KY.

Pickens, W. H. (1982, December). *Performance funding in higher education: Panacea or peril?* Paper presented at a Conference on Survival in the 1980s. Quality, Mission and Financing Options. Tucson, AZ. (ED 236 980)

Piturro, M. (1999). Alternatives to downsizing. *Management Review, 88*(9), 37–41.

Plater, W. (1995). Future work: Faculty time in the 21st century. *Change, 27,* 22–33.

Presley, J. B., & Engelbride, E. (1998). Accounting for faculty productivity in the research university. *Review of Higher Education, 22*(1), 17–37.

Press, E., & Washburn, J. (2000, March). The kept university. *The Atlantic Monthly* [On-line]. Available: http://www.theatlantic.com/issues/2000

Qayoumi, M. H. (1999). Utilities metering and measurement. *Facilities Manager, 15*(2), 30–36.

Raiford, R. (1998, November). High-tech, high-touch learning. *Buildings Interior, 2*(5), 4–8.

Rankin, J. (2000). A decade of restructuring at Merian library, California State University, Chico. *The Bottom Line: Managing Library Finances, 13*(1), 26–33.

Rea, J. W. (1998, March). A core collection strategy for protecting undergraduate education at a comprehensive university. *Journal of Academic Librarianship, 24*(2), 145–150.

Reindl, T. (1998). *State and national issues affecting public higher education. Deferred maintenance.* Compendium of AASCU Special Reports. (ED 421 036)

Richardson, R. C., Bracco, K., Callan, P., & Finney, J. E. (1998). *Higher education governance: Balancing institutional and market influences.* San Jose, CA: National Center for Public Policy and Higher Education. (ED 426 641)

Rose, R. (1999). *Charting a new course for campus renewal. Lesson from the New Mexico higher education symposium on capital renewal and deferred maintenance.* Alexandria, VA: Association of Higher Education Facilities Officers. (ED 435 287)

Rosenzweig, M. (1998). *The political university: Policy, politics, and presidential leadership in the American Research University.* Baltimore: The Johns Hopkins University Press. (ED 416 761)

Rourke, F., & Brooks, G. (1966). *The managerial revolution in higher education.* Baltimore: The Johns Hopkins University Press.

Ruppert, S. S. (1995). Roots and realities of state-level performance indicator system. In G. H. Gaither (Ed.), *Assessing performance in an age of accountability: Case studies.* New Directions for Higher Education, no. 91. San Francisco: Jossey-Bass.

Ruppert, S. S. (1998). *Focus on the customer: A new approach to state-level accountability reporting and processes for higher education.* Denver, CO: State Higher Education Executive Officers. (ED 421 063)

Rush, S. C. (1991). Managing the facilities portfolio: New book addresses elimination of $60 billion problem. *Business Officer, 24*(9), 26–28.

Rush, S. C. (1994). Contracting for facilities services. Critical Issues in Facilities Management, no. 9. Alexandria, VA: Association of Higher Education Facilities Officers. (ED 408 872)

Rush, S. C. (1994). To contract or not to contract is not the question. *Trusteeship, 2*(4), 11–16.

Rush, S. C., & Johnson, S. L. (1989). *The decaying American campus: A ticking time bomb.* Alexandria, VA: Association of Higher Education Facilities Officers.

Saltzman, G. M. (2000). Union organizing and the law: Part-time faculty and graduate teaching assistants. *NEA almanac of higher education.* Washington, DC: National Education Association.

Sanders, J. (1997, February 9). Debate over college tenure dividing America: The public and the professorate regard each other less warmly. *News & Record,* Greensboro, N.C., p. F3.

Sanville, T. (1999). Use levels and new models for consortia purchasing of electronic journals. *Library Consortium Management, 1*(34).

Schaeffer, S. C. (1999). Electric deregulation: Don't get the cart before the horse. *Facilities Manager, 15*(2) 39–41.

Schaeffner, R. (1997-1998, Winter). Recovering from sputnik. *Planning for Higher Education, 26,* 27–31.

Schmidt, P. (1998). A building boom for public colleges. *The Chronicle of Higher Education, 44*(40), A29–A30.

Schneider, K. G. (1998, January). The McLibrary syndrome. *American Libraries, 29*(1), 66–70.

Schroeder, R. (1995, Summer). Access vs. owner in academic libraries. *Katharine Sharp Review,* (1) [On-line]. Available: http://www.lisuiuc.edu/review/summer1995/ schroeder.html

Schubbe, T. L. (1999). Utility management in the 21st century: Challenges and opportunities. *Facilities Manager, 15*(2), 15–21.

Schuman, P. G. (1998, August). The selling of the public library: It's not just outsourcing, it's privatization. *Library Journal, 123,* 13, 50–52.

Serban, A. M. (1998). Precursor of performance funding. In J. C. Burke and A. M. Serban (Eds.), *Performance funding for public higher education: Fad or trend?* (pp. 15–21). New Directions for Institutional Research, no. 97. San Francisco: Jossey-Bass.

Sharper, L. (1997, April 24). Tenure comes under stricter review. *Christian Science Monitor,* p. 12.

Shaw, R. (1988, December 19). Helping the underperformer shed the under. *Hotel & Motel Management, 203,* 40, 42.

Shils, E. (1995, April 18). (Qtd in Gerhard Casper), *Come the millennium, Where the university?* Keynote address, American Educational Research Association annual meeting, San Francisco, CA.

Shirley, R. C. (1994). *Strategic and operational reform in public higher education: A mandate for change.* Washington, DC: Association of Governing Boards of Universities and Colleges. (ED 412 848)

Simko. E. A. (1990). *Creating funding of energy conservation projects. Critical Issues in Facilities Management.* Alexandria, VA: Association of Physical Plant Administrators of Universities and Colleges.

Simon, M. (1997). One university's experience starting fee-based information systems: Two case studies from UNLV. *The Bottom Line: Managing Library Finances, 10*(4), 153–157.

Simpson, W. B. (1991). *Cost containment for higher education: Strategies for public policy and institutional administration.* New York: Praeger.

Sizer, J. (1989). *Performance indicators and quality control in higher education.* Keynote Address to an International Conference, Institute of Education, London.

Slaughter, S., & Leslie, L. (1997). *Academic capitalism: Politics, policy and the entrepreneurial University.* Baltimore: The Johns Hopkins University Press.

Sloan, B. (1998). Allocating costs in a consortia environment: A methodology for library consortia. *The Bottom Line: Managing Library Finances, 11*(2), 65–72.

South Carolina Commission on Higher Education. (1992, June 4). *South Carolina higher education. Deferred maintenance problems 1981–1991.* Columbia, SC: South Carolina Commission on Higher Education. (ED 350 942)

South Carolina Commission on Higher Education. (1997). *Minding Our "P"s and "Q"s: Indication of productivity and quality in South Carolina's public colleges and universities. Report on Act 255 of 1992 and Summary Report on Institutional Effectiveness.* Columbia, SC: South Carolina Commission on Higher Education. (ED 404 963)

Standards for College Libraries. (1986, March). American library association and association of college and research libraries. *News, 47*(3), 189–200.

State Issues Digest. (1999). American Association of State Colleges and Universities.

State of New York Office of the State Comptroller, Division of Management Audit. (1992, December 15). *State of New York Staff Study Regarding the Effectiveness of the University's Energy Conservation Program.* (ED 353 877)

State University of New York. New York Office of the Comptroller. (1991). *Facility utilization. Are faculty workloads reasonable and cost effective?* (ED 344 563)

Stepp, Joe Alan. President, Alice Lloyd College [On-line]. Available: http://ww4.choice.net?-taulbee/alc.html

Stevens, J., & Hamlett, B. D. (1983). State concerns for learning: Quality and state policy. In *Meeting the New Demands or Standards* (29–37). New Directions for Higher Education, no. 43.

St. John, E. P. (1994). *Prices, productivity, and investment: Assessing financial strategies in higher education.* ASHE-ERIC Higher Education Report, no. 3. Washington, DC: The George Washington University. (ED 382 093. 171 pp. MF-01; PC-07)

Stoller, M. A., Christopherson, R., & Miranda, M. (1996). The economics of professional journal pricing. *Colleges and Research Libraries, 57*(1), 9–21.

Sturgeon, J. (1998). Getting the most from your on-line energy management system. *College Planning & Management, 1*(1), 63–65.

Suber, L. T. (1982, May). Coping with deferred maintenance. *Business Officer, 22–24.* (ED 226 622)

Swistock, R. J. (1996). *Change to zone maintenance.* Proceeding of the 1996 Educational Conference and 83rd Annual Meeting, July 21–23, 1996. Salt Lake City, Utah.

Tallman, I., & Ward, D. A. (1997, July 27). The great tenure debate: No they don't. *The Washington Post,* R1.

Taylor, B. E., & Massy, W. F. (1996). *Strategic indicators for higher education: Vital benchmarks and information to help you evaluate and improve your institution's performance.* Princeton, NJ: Peterson Guides, 1996.

Texas Higher Education Coordinating Board. (1996, July 31). *Facilities fact book, 1995. Texas public universities, health related institutions and technical colleges.* Austin, TX: Texas Higher Education Coordination Board. Campus Planning Office. (ED 401 800)

Thomson, A. A., & Strickland. (1995). *Strategic management. Concepts and cases.* Chicago: Irwin.

Tierney, W. G. (1998). Leveling tenure: Locating tenure and other controversies. *American Behavioral Scientist, 41*(5), 627–637.

U.S. Department of Energy. (1996, September). *An analysis of FERC's final environmental impact statement for electricity: Open access and recovery of stranded costs.* Washington, DC: Office of Integrated Analysis and Forecasting.

Vandament, W. (1989). *Finance management in higher education.* San Francisco: Jossey-Bass.

Vanderheiden, P., De Meuse, K., Bergman, P., & Thomas, J. (1999). Response to Haar's comment—and the beat goes on: Corporate downsizing in the twenty-first century. *Human Resource Management, 38*(3), 261–267.

Van Dusen, G. C. (1997). *The virtual campus: Technology and reform in higher education.* ASHE-ERIC Higher Education Report, no. 5. Washington DC: The George Washington University. (ED 412 816. 191 pp. MF-01; PC-08)

Virginia Higher Education. (1991, July 10). *Colleges and universities for the 21st century: A report and proposals for continued improvement in Virginia higher education.* Richmond, VA: Virginia State Council on Higher Education.

Waggaman, J. S. (1991). *Strategies and consequences: Managing the costs in higher education.* ASHE-ERIC Higher Education Report, no. 8. Washington, DC: The George Washington University, School of Education and Human Development.

Walters, L. R. (1997, April 24). Tenure comes under strict review. *The Christian Science Monitor.*

Walsh, J. T. (1992). *State University of New York—staff study regarding the effectiveness of the university's energy conservation program (Report 93-D5).* Albany, NY: State University of New York. (ED 353 877)

Wergin, J. F. (1994). *The collaboration department: How five campuses are inching toward cultures of collective responsibility. Forum on faculty roles & rewards.* Washington DC: American Association of Higher Education. (ED 406 958)

Wertz, R. D. (1997, Winter). Big business on campus: Examining the bottom line. *Educational Record, 78*(1), 19–24.

Western Interstate Commission on Higher Education (1998). *Knocking at the door: Projections of high school graduates by state and race/ethnicity 1996–2012.* Boulder, CO.

Weston, J. F., Jawien, P. S., & Levitas, E. J. (1998, January). Restructuring and its implication for business economics. *Business Economics, 33*(1), 41–46.

Whalen, E. L. (1991). *Responsibility centered budgeting. An approach to decentralized management for institutions of higher education.* Bloomington, IN: Indiana University Press.

Wheeler, W. J. (2000). Scanning book tables of contents: A preliminary report on costs and procedures. *The Bottom Line: Managing Library Finances, 13*(1), 21–25.

Whisler, S., & Rosenblatt, S. (1997). *The library and the university press: Two views of the costs and problems of the current system of scholarly publishing.* Paper presented at the Conference on Scholarly Communications and Technology, April 24–25, 1997. Atlanta, Georgia [On-line]. Available: http.//www.arl.org/scomm/scat (ED 414 921)

White, H. (2000). Why outsourcing happens and what to do about it. *American Libraries, 31*(1), 66–71.

Wilhoit, K. (1994). Outsourcing cataloging at Wright State University. *Serials Review, 20,* 70–73.

Wilson, R. (1999, October 22). How a university created 95 faculty slots and scaled back its use of part-timers. *The Chronicle of Higher Education, 46* [On-line]. Available: http://chronicle.com

Wilson, R. (1998, June 12). Contracts replace the tenure track for growing number of professors. *The Chronicle of Higher Education, 44* [On-line]. Available: http://chronicle.com

Wingspread Group on Higher Education. (1993). *An American imperative: Higher expectations for higher education.* Racine, WI: The Johnson Foundation.

Winston, G. C. (1997). Why can't a college be more like a firm? *Change, 29*(5), 32–38.

Winston, G. C. (1994, September/October). The decline in undergraduate teaching. *Change, 26*(5), 8–15.

Wittenberg, R. C. (1996). Reengineering and the approval plan: New process or new perspective? *The Acquisitions Librarian, 16,* 61.

Wittorf, R. (1998). Outsourcing photocopying in a library: One experience. *The Bottom Line: Managing Library Finances, 11*(3), 101–104.

Yarmolinsky, A. (1996, May/June). Tenure: Permanence and change; academic tenure. *Change, 28*(3), 16–20.

Yeoman, B., Palani, M. M., & McKee, John, C. (1998). Assessment and utilities savings at UT Houston. *Facilities Manager, 14*(3), 17–20, 22.

Yudof, M. (1992, May 13). The Burgeoning privatization of state universities. *The Chronicle of Higher Education,* A48.

Zappan, S. (1996). Two libraries, one direction. *The Bottom Line: Managing Library Finances, 9*(2), 21–27.

Zemsky, R. (1993). Toward restructuring: Assessing the impact of budgeting constraints on college and university operations. *Policy Perspectives, 4*(4), 7B–16B.

Zemsky, R., & Massey, W. F. (1990). *The dynamics of academic productivity.* Report from Denver College. Seminar Transcript, State Higher Education Executive Officers Association.

Zemsky, R., & Massey, W. F. (1990, November/December). Cost containment in the new reality. *Change, 22,* 16–22.

Zeloznicki, S. (2000). Do you need an energy master plan? *College Planning & Management, 3*(7), 39–40.

Zumeta, W., & Fawcett-Long, J. (1996). State budget developments. *NEA almanac of higher education.* Washington, DC: National Education Association.

Zumeta, W. (2000). Accountability: Challenges for higher education. *NEA almanac of higher education.* Washington, DC: National Education Association.

Zumeta, W. (2001). Public policy and accountability in higher education: Lessons from the past and present for the new millennium. In D. E. Heller (Ed.), *The states and public higher education policy: Affordability, access and accountability* (pp. 155–197). Baltimore: The Johns Hopkins University Press.

Name Index

Abel-Kops, C., 43
Ahumada, M. M., 110
Allen, H., 14
Anderson, R. E., 2
Angell, M., 82
Ashworth, K. W., 113
Astin, A. W., 95–96, 103
Astle, D., 34

Balderston, F. E., 110
Baldwin, R. G., 28
Basheda, G., 68
Battin, P., 31
Baughman, J. C., 26
Benjamin, R., 122, 123, 124
Berdahl, R. O., 101–102
Bergman, P., 25
Berne, R., 2
Bero, L. A., 77
Biddison, G. B., 57
Blumenstyk, G., 76, 82
Boatright, K. J., 106–108
Boer, W. J., 86–87
Bogue, G. E., 102
Bok, D., 140
Boutwell, W. K., 110
Bowen, H. R., 138, 141
Bracco, K., 99
Brainard, J., 78
Brawer, F. B., 94
Breneman, D. W., 121
Brennan, E., 119
Breslin, R. D., 139
Brinkman, P. T., 141
Brown, J. R., 13
Brown, S. L., 60, 61
Brownstein, A., 136, 139
Bucklin, L. P., 13
Burgan, M., 26
Burke, J., 112, 117

Callan, P., 99
Carlson, T. R., 9
Carnevale, D., 86, 88
Carrol, S., 122, 123, 124
Carter, K., 113
Cartwright, C., 18–19, 19, 20
Casper, G., 136
Caudle, D. M., 44
Cave, M., 103
Chait, R., 2, 24, 26
Champy, J., 119
Cho, M., 77
Christopherson, R., 33, 36
Chronister, J. L., 8, 9, 12, 28
Clark, M. C., 13
Clery, S. B., 7
Clotfelter, C. T., 141
Cohen, C. M., 16, 17
Cole, J., 99
Coll, M., 94
Cordes, C., 78
Crow, M. M., 76
Curry, J. A., 121

Davies, E., 37
DeHayes, D. W., 117–120
Delano, D., 9
Demeuse, K, 25
Derlin, R., 102
Dev, C. S., 13
Diamond, R. M., 2
Dickmeyer, N., 111
Dill, D., 102–103
Dochy, F.J.R.C., 113
Duchin, D., 44–46
Duffey, J. D., 71–72
Dwyer, J., 39

Ehrenberg, R. G., 24, 27, 80,
   90–91

El-Khawas, E., 18, 121, 122
Engelbride, E., 14
English, R., 33
Epstein, G., 25
Ewing, K., 21

Fairweather, J., 16
Fawcett-Long, J., 100
Fickes, M., 53–54
Figg, J., 55, 57
Filippello, A. N., 120
Finney, J. E., 99
Flanagan, J. S., 49, 52,
   54–55
Folger, J., 111
Fonte, R., 101
Ford, A. T., 2
Fox-Penner, P., 68
Frank, R. H., 90–91, 91
Freeman, T., 105
Frost, S. H., 94

Gappa, J. M., 2, 10
Garland, P. H., 86, 96
Gaylord, T. A., 125–127
Getz, M., 36, 57
Giffin, R. E., 59
Gilbert, S. W., 17
Givens, L., 62
Glassick, C. E., 71
Glenny, L. A., 99
Gobstein, H., 80
Goldman, R. N., 26
Goldstein, P. J., 57
Goodman, D., 34
Gose, B., 56
Goudy, F., 32
Grace, T. W., 86, 96
Green, K. C., 17, 18
Grimm, J. C., 53–54

Subject Index

outsourcing as, 43–44; restructure of tenure as, 27–28; of state legislatures, 2; for technology use, 39; workforce reduction as, 26
Council for Aid to Education, 2
Curriculum duplication, 16–17

Deferred maintenance, 50–55, 69, 131
Deregulation of utility industry, 59–61, 132
Digital material, 34, 38, 40–43
Diversity, 104

Earmarked appropriations, 78
Eastern Washington University, 34–35, 47
Education Amendments (1972), 88–89
Effectiveness, 104
Efficiency, 104, 127, 134
Electricity, 59, 132
Electronic material. *See* Digital material
Emmanuel College, 96
Employee Benefits Research Institute, 9
Energy management: deregulation and, 59–61, 65–68, 132; electricity and, 59; Green Lights program for, 60; master utility plan and, 62; overview of, 59, 69; at State University of New York, 63–65; stranded cost and, 61; utility supplier and, 60–61
Energy Policy Act (1992), 60
Enrollment, increases in, 100–101
Evaluation of project cost, 53–54
Executive Order No. 177, 107

Facilities. *See* Plant operations
Facilities maintenance plan, 54
Faculty: budget education and, 79–80; full-time, 10, 27, 28, 129; input into cost containment, 139; mandatory retirement and, 11; part-time, 10–11, 129; research priority of, 74; rewards for, 75–76; tenure–accomplishment

relationship and, 28; tenured, 11–12, 130; tenured versus contract, 27; two-tiered system of, 27; view of productivity, 15, 129; workload of, 74
Faculty compensation: academic discipline and, 8; average of, 7; benefits and, 8; for full-time faculty, 10; geographic location and, 7–8; retirement packages as, 11–12; total expenditure for, 29. *See also* Instructional costs
Faculty productivity: class size and, 13, 14, 15; consortia arrangements and, 17; curriculum duplication and, 16–17; faculty definition versus conventional measures, 13; instruction versus research issue and, 15–16; issues with, 14, 129–130; at Kent State University, 18–23; measurement of, 12–13, 14, 15; recommendations for, 16–18; research publications and, 13; state legislatures and, 14; study of, 20
Federal regulations, 88–89
Financial aid: elite universities and, 90–92; federal regulations and, 88; grants versus loans, 90, 92; increase in, 136; minority students and, 90; overview of, 89; tuition and, 89
Florida, 100
Florida State Postsecondary Commission, 105
Formula-based budgets, 109–110
Freeport McMoRan, 77
Fringe benefits, 8
Funding: competition for, 75–76; decision making process for, 101, 127; performance funding, 112–119, 127–128, 135; state appropriations as, 100, 127. *See also* Research

Government regulations, 77–78, 83
Governor's Commission, 115

Graduate programs, 81
Graduation rates, 17
Grants. *See* Funding; Research
Green Lights program, 60

Harvard Business Review, 4
Health care plans, 9–10
Higher Education Restructuring Act, 122

Illinois Board of Higher Education, 52, 109
Incremental budgets, 108–110
Indiana University, 117–119
Instruction versus research, 15–16
Instructional costs: collective bargaining and, 10; increases in, 7; mandatory retirement and, 11; state legislatures and, 2; tenure as, 2. *See also* Faculty compensation
Insurance, medical, 8

Johns Hopkins University Press, 40
Joint Commission on Accountability Reporting
Journal STORrage project (JSTOR), 39
Journal subscriptions, 31–32, 33–36
Journals, 31–32, 33–36, 40–43

K-Mart, 77
Kent State University, 18–23
Kentucky General Assembly, 116
Kentucky University, 114–117

Mandatory retirement, 11
Manhattan College, 10
Maricopa County Community College District, 63
Maryland Higher Education Commission, 15, 16, 104–105, 134
Massachusetts College of Pharmacy and Allied Health Services, 96
Master utility plan, 62
Medical insurance, 8
Milton S. Eisenhower Library, 40
Minority students, 90
Mission of universities, 72–73
Mississippi, 100

Montana University System, 124–125
Montana University System Board of Regents, 124–125

"A Nation at Risk," 102
National Academy of Sciences, 82
National Center for Educational Statistics, 7
National Center on Postsecondary Teaching, Learning, and Assessment, 16
National Commission on the Cost of Higher Education, 1, 2–3
National Education Association, 7–8, 10
National Labor Relations Board, 10
Nelson A. Rockefeller Institute of Government, 112
New Jersey, 11, 121
New Jersey Commission on Higher Education, 122
New Mexico Commission on Higher Education, 109
New York, 66–67
New York University, 11

Office of Admissions, 87
Office of the Registrar, 87
OPACs, 37
Orientation programs, 93–94
Outsourcing: in libraries, 43–47, 48, 130–131; overview of, 133; for plant operations, 55–59, 69, 133; for student services, 96–97

Patents, 76
Peer review, 78
Pennsylvania, 67–68
Performance-based budgeting, 112–115, 128, 135
Performance funding, 111–120, 127–128, 135
Performance indicators, 104–105, 127, 134
Plant operations: deferred maintenance and, 50–55, 69, 131; energy management, 59–68, 132; expenditure overview, 49; 1980s fiscal crisis and, 49–50; outsourcing for, 133;

research and, 80; strategic plans, 53
Policy makers, 101, 113, 127
Portfolio, facility, 53
Princeton University, 92
Private universities: benefit costs, 8; deferred maintenance and, 51; faculty sharing of, 17; instructional costs of, 7; tuition of, 1, 86
Productivity. *See* Faculty productivity
Professionalism, 55
Program budgeting, 109–111
Project MUSE, 40
Public image of universities, 85
Public universities. *See* State universities
Publishers, journal, 33–34

Quality, 104, 127

Rehabilitation Act (1973), 88
Remediation, student, 95–96
Report of the National Commission on the Cost of Higher Education, 2–3
Research: absorption of costs of, 79; commercialization of, 75–77, 81–82; competition for funding of, 75–76; earmarked appropriations and, 78; evaluating role of, 72; as faculty priority, 74; faculty rewards and, 75–76; graduate programs and, 81; grant requirements for, 77–78, 83; historical overview, 71; indirect costs of, 77–78; versus instruction, 15–16; peer review of, 78; plant operations and, 80; promotional techniques for, 80–81; rewards for, 133; undergraduates for, 81; university mission and, 72–73; university–corporate partnership, 81–82
Research publications, 13
Responsibility-centered management, 117–119
Responsibility-centered budgeting, 111, 135
Restructuring initiatives, 119–127, 128, 135

Retirement, 8, 11–12
Royalties, 76

San Diego State University, 63
Scott Paper, 120–121
Sears, Roebuck and Co., 120
Simmons College, 96
Social Security, 8
South Carolina, 105
South Carolina Commission on Higher Education, 53, 105
Southern Methodist University, 38–39
Standards for College Libraries, 32
Stanford University, 59
State coordinating boards, 122
State Issues Digest, 112, 114
State legislatures: cost containment strategies of, 2; faculty productivity and, 14; instructional costs and, 2; utility deregulation and, 65–68
State universities: benefit costs of, 8; deferred maintenance and, 51; faculty sharing of, 17; instructional costs of, 7; tuition of, 1, 85–86
State University of New York, 63–65
States: assessment and, 102, 103–108, 127; economic growth of, 100, 126; governing structures of, 101; performance funding and, 112–115, 127–128; university accountability and, 102–108, 127; university restructuring and, 120–125, 128
Stevens Institute of Technology, 40–43
Strategic plans: academic libraries and, 39; academic support prioritization and, 38; benefits of, 140; plant operations and, 53; restructuring and, 123; student services and, 86–87; at University of Texas (Houston), 63
Student activities, 93–94
Student attrition, 93–94
Student preparedness, 95, 134
Student services: academic advising as, 94; consortia for,

ASHE-ERIC
Higher Education Reports

The mission of the Educational Resources Information Center (ERIC) system is to improve American education by increasing and facilitating the use of educational research and information on practice in the activities of learning, teaching, educational decision making, and research, wherever and whenever these activities take place.

Since 1983, the ASHE-ERIC Higher Education Report series has been published in cooperation with the Association for the Study of Higher Education (ASHE). Starting in 2000, the series has been published by Jossey-Bass in conjunction with the ERIC Clearinghouse on Higher Education.

Each monograph is the definitive analysis of a tough higher education problem, based on thorough research of pertinent literature and institutional experiences. Topics are identified by a national survey. Noted practitioners and scholars are then commissioned to write the reports, with experts providing critical reviews of each manuscript before publication.

Six monographs in the series are published each year and are available on individual and subscription bases. To order, use the order form at the back of this issue.

Qualified persons interested in writing a monograph for the series are invited to submit a proposal to the National Advisory Board. As the preeminent literature review and issue analysis series in higher education, the Higher Education Reports are guaranteed wide dissemination and provide national exposure for accepted candidates. Execution of a monograph requires at least a minimal familiarity with the ERIC database, including *Resources in Education* and the current *Index to Journals in Education*. The objective of these reports is to bridge conventional wisdom and practical research.

Advisory Board

Review Panelists and Consulting Editors

Paul Chewning
Council for Advancement and
Support of Education

Donald Heller
University of Michigan

Christopher Morphew
University of Kansas

Edward P. St. John
Indiana University

Richard C. Richardson, Jr.
New York University

Mark Oromaner
Hudson County Community
College

Richard Alfred
University of Michigan

Recent Titles

Volume 28 ASHE-ERIC Higher Education Reports

1. The Changing Nature of the Academic Deanship
   Mimi Wolverton, Walter H. Gmelch, Joni Montez, and Charles T. Nies

2. Faculty Compensation Systems: Impact on the Quality of Higher Education
   Terry P. Sutton, Peter J. Bergerson

3. Socialization of Graduate and Professional Students in Higher Education:
   A Perilous Passage?
   John C. Weidman, Darla J. Twale, Elizabeth Leahy Stein

4. Understanding and Facilitating Organizational Change in the 21st Century: Recent
   Research and Conceptualizations
   Adrianna J. Kezar

Volume 27 ASHE-ERIC Higher Education Reports

1. The Art and Science of Classroom Assessment: The Missing Part of Pedagogy
   Susan M. Brookhart

2. Due Process and Higher Education: A Systemic Approach to Fair Decision Making
   Ed Stevens

3. Grading Students' Classroom Writing: Issues and Strategies
   Bruce W. Speck

4. Posttenure Faculty Development: Building a System for Faculty Improvement
   and Appreciation
   Jeffrey W. Alstete

5. Digital Dilemma: Issues of Access, Cost, and Quality in Media-Enhanced and Distance
   Education
   Gerald C. Van Dusen

6. Women and Minority Faculty in the Academic Workplace: Recruitment, Retention, and
   Academic Culture
   Adalberto Aguirre, Jr.

7. Higher Education Outside of the Academy
   Jeffrey A. Cantor

8. Academic Departments: How They Work, How They Change
   *Barbara E. Walvoord, Anna K. Carey, Hoke L. Smith, Suzanne W. Soled,
   Philip K. Way, Debbie Zorn*

Back Issue/Subscription Order Form

Copy or detach and send to:
Jossey-Bass, 989 Market Street, San Francisco, CA 94103-1741

Call or fax toll free!
Phone 888-378-2537 6AM-5PM PST; Fax 800-605-2665

Individual reports:	Please send me the following reports at $24 each (Important: please include series initials and issue number, such as AEHE 27:1)

1. AEHE _____

_____

_____

$ _____ Total for individual reports

$ _____ Shipping charges (for individual reports *only;* subscriptions are exempt from shipping charges): Up to $30, add $5^{50} • $30^{01}–$50, add $6^{50} $50^{01}–$75, add $8 • $75^{01}–$100, add $10 • $100^{01}–$150, add $12 Over $150, call for shipping charge

Subscriptions   Please ❑ start my subscription to *ASHE-ERIC Higher Education Reports* at the following rate (6 issues):
U.S.: $130   Canada: $130   All others: $178

$ _____ Total individual reports and subscriptions (Add appropriate sales tax for your state for individual reports. No sales tax on U.S. subscriptions. Canadian residents, add GST for subscriptions and individual reports.)

Federal Tax ID 135593032   GST 89102-8052

❑ Payment enclosed (U.S. check or money order only)
❑ VISA, MC, AmEx, Discover Card # _____ Exp. date _____

Signature _____ Day phone _____
❑ Bill me (U.S. institutional orders only. Purchase order required.)
Purchase order #_____

Name _____

Address _____

_____

Phone_____ E-mail _____

For more information about Jossey-Bass, visit our Web site at:
www.josseybass.com   **PRIORITY CODE = ND1**

WALTER A. BROWN is assistant professor of higher education administration at The George Washington University's Graduate School of Education and Human Development. His research interests include finance in higher education, strategic planning, and adapting the business paradigm to higher education administration. He has substantial experience in the corporate finance sector from working for such companies as The Bank of New York, Avon Products Inc., and PepsiCo Inc. He has also worked as a professional staff member on the Budget Committee, United States House of Representatives prior to joining the ranks of higher education. He received his doctorate in higher education administration from The George Washington University.

CAYO GAMBER is assistant professor of English at The George Washington University. She earned her B.A. at the College of William and Mary and has earned an M. Phil, a Ph.D. in Literature, and an Ed.S. in higher education administration at The George Washington University. In her recent research, she has analyzed the use of technology in the classroom, the contested place of tenure in the academy, and the changing role of women in higher education. She currently teaches in the Department of English, the Women's Studies Program, and the Humanities Program at The George Washington University.